Ugly as Sin

A Forthright Edition™

Sophia Institute Press awards the privileged title "A Forthright Edition" to a select few of our books that address contemporary Catholic issues with clarity, cogency, and force, and that are also destined to become classics for all times.

> Forthright Editions are *direct*, explaining their principles briefly, simply, and clearly to Catholics in the pews, on whom the future of the Church depends. The time for ambiguity or confusion is past.

> Forthright Editions are *contemporary*, born of our own time and circumstances and intended to become significant voices in current debates, voices that serious Catholics cannot ignore, regardless of their prior views.

> Forthright Editions are *classical*, addressing themes and enunciating principles that are valid for all ages and cultures. Readers will turn to them time and again for guidance in other days and different circumstances.

> Forthright Editions are *charitable*, entering contemporary debates solely in order to clarify basic issues and to demonstrate how those issues can be resolved in a way that strengthens souls and the Church.

Please feel free to suggest topics and authors for future Forthright Editions. And please pray that Forthright Editions may help to resolve the crisis of the Church in our day.

Michael S. Rose

Ugly as Sin

Why They Changed Our Churches
from Sacred Places to Meeting Spaces —
and How We Can Change Them Back Again

SOPHIA INSTITUTE PRESS®
Manchester, New Hampshire

Sophia Institute Press®
Box 5284, Manchester, NH 03108
1-800-888-9344
www.sophiainstitute.com

Library of Congress Cataloging-in-Publication Data

Rose, Michael S., 1969-
    Ugly as sin : why they changed our churches from sacred places to meeting spaces and how we can change them back again / Michael S. Rose.
        p.   cm.
    Includes bibliographical references.
    ISBN 1-928832-36-9 (alk. paper)
    1. Catholic church buildings. 2. Church architecture — 20th century. I. Title.

NA4828 .R67 2001
246'.9582'09045 — dc21   2001049617

01 02 03 04 05 06 07 08 09 10 9 8 7 6 5 4 3 2 1

Contents

Appendix

Foreword

Why do the Catholic churches built over the past three or four decades look the way they do? Why are they so different from churches of past ages, which all seemed to be built in a similar arrangement, using familiar elements and forms most people immediately associate with a church building? Why are our modern churches so ugly, so banal, so uninspiring?

Is it just a matter of taste?

Or is something more fundamental at stake?

To many people, these questions seem as unanswerable as they are mysterious. *Ugly as Sin* answers these hard questions and shows how Catholics can — and must — return to building sacred places worthy of the title "house of God."

Modern church architect Edward A. Sövik underscores this point when he writes that "architecture is a more influential factor in the life of society than most people suppose."[1] Church architecture affects the way man worships; the way he worships affects what he believes; and what he believes affects not only his personal relationship with God but how he conducts himself in his daily life.

---

[1] E. A. Sövik, *Architecture for Worship* (Minneapolis: Augsburg Publishing House, 1973), 19.

In other words, church architecture is not negligible but significant, not the concern only of architects but central to your life and mine. The elements of our churches express a theology, manifest a particular Faith. Contrast the Quaker meetinghouse with a Gothic cathedral, and you must conclude that these two buildings represent two distinct theologies, two distinct ecclesiologies, two very different ways of looking at the Church founded by Jesus Christ.

Successful, authentic church architecture reflects the doctrines of the faith it represents. A Gothic cathedral no more reflects the faith of the Quakers than the Quaker meetinghouse reflects the truths of the Catholic Faith. What, then, can we say about modern Catholic church architecture?

That's the topic of this book, which is more about architectural theology than it is about church architecture per se. But don't be intimidated by the term *architectural theology*. It simply means that church architecture is more than a matter of taste and more than a matter of tradition: what we build as a house of God should reflect what we believe about God.

The basics aren't hard to understand. Once you grasp them, you'll understand why modern Catholic churches have deviated from the natural laws of Catholic church architecture to take the often bland and grotesque shape that they have.

And you'll know why it's so important that we return to those natural laws that guided church builders of old, leading them to create churches that lift the soul to God by authentically representing the Catholic Faith.

Michael S. Rose

Ugly as Sin

Chapter One

⌒

The three natural laws of church architecture
(or, the minimum you need to know
to evaluate the church down the street)

Notre Dame, the crowning jewel of Paris, is arguably the most famous of Christendom's great cathedral churches. Countless chronicles, poems, novels, and artistic treatments have been devoted to the subject of this architectural masterpiece. Yet considering it's neither the tallest, the biggest, nor even the most beautiful of cathedrals, Notre Dame's universal appeal isn't easily explicable on the natural order.

There's something more.

Paris, of course, as the capital of France, provides a prominent setting not enjoyed by most churches, yet it's the building's own transcendent qualities that have led countless pilgrims from all parts of the world to marvel at its presence and enter into its sublimity. "Itinerant merchants and priests, pilgrims, diplomats, foreign students, traveling knights and crusaders, freed serfs seeking new homes — the whole wandering human fabric of the Middle Ages passed through the capital of France and admired its Cathedral." So reports Allan Temko in his 1955 book on Notre Dame.[2]

[2]   Allan Temko, *Notre-Dame of Paris: The Biography of a Cathedral* (New York: Viking Press, 1955), 136.

These pilgrims, he adds, called Notre Dame the *ecclesia* of Paris, the church par excellence in a city of many remarkable churches. And since that time long ago, pilgrims and tourists have never ceased to come to this heart of medieval Paris on the *Île de la Cité*.

The grand church is no mere icon for the city, as we might say of the Eiffel Tower or even the great Arc de Triomphe. Rather, it's truly the epicenter — the soul — of one of the great cities of Christendom. In 1902, Hilaire Belloc even described sprawling Paris as the fringe of the great cathedral's garment. He spoke of the church in distinctly human terms: as a lady in a great house who is the center of the estate.

Nearly a century earlier, in his novel about the hunchbacked bell-ringer of the great Notre Dame, Victor Hugo, too, personified the cathedral, although in a more indirect and symbolic way. In Hugo's novel *The Hunchback of Notre Dame*, Quasimodo the bell-ringer represents that maternal bond of intimacy between man and the Church, and ultimately between man and God. To this hunchback, Notre Dame is egg, nest, home, country, and universe, just as is the Church universal for all the baptized.

When still a child, Quasimodo dragged himself through the cathedral, wrote Hugo, as if he were "some reptile native to that damp, dark pavement upon which the Roman capitals cast so many grotesque shadows."[3] Indeed, Notre Dame was the hunchback's dwelling, his wrapper, peopled with marble figures — kings, saints, and bishops — who blessed him and looked upon him with goodwill. In a certain sense, Hugo depicts this "dwelling place" as a living, breathing soul prepared for the intimacy of mere mortals — a view all the more remarkable since Hugo had more of a revolutionary mind than a Christian one. Nevertheless, whether Hugo knew it or not, the great cathedral of Notre Dame transcended his own world view. He could not escape the "other-worldly" character

[3] Victor Hugo, *The Hunchback of Notre Dame* (1831), 183.

Built over nine decades, from 1163 to 1250, the Parisian
Notre Dame is noted for its verticality, permanence, and iconography.

Standing in the cathedral plaza, the pilgrim comes face-to-face with Notre Dame's awe-evoking western façade, which is so familiar to us today.

of this great church, and he admits that he gave himself up to a power and order greater than himself. In short, Hugo encountered, however unwittingly, a foretaste of the heavenly Jerusalem.

Throughout the Christian centuries, the church building has been understood to be what Notre Dame exemplifies so well: the *domus Dei* ("house of God") and the *porta coeli* ("gate of Heaven"), that dwelling place where we go to find God, that sacred place in which we seek the treasures of the heavenly kingdom. Ever since the days when King Solomon received the commission directly from God to fashion the holy temple, men of every epoch have toiled and labored with devout hands and have spared no resources to build such splendid palaces for the King of Kings.

Built over nine decades, from 1163 to 1250, the Parisian Notre Dame, noted for its elegant proportions, served as a model for the many Gothic cathedrals that were built in northern France in the thirteenth century. Inside and out, the building has inspired countless pilgrims over the centuries. Each has approached the cathedral from one of Paris's many streets or along the quays of the Left Bank, catching glimpses of the tall towers from afar and, later, in the cathedral plaza, standing face-to-face with the awe-evoking Western façade that's so familiar to most of us today. Yet even the familiarity acquired from a distance through travel guides, textbooks, magazine articles, movies, and even cartoons doesn't detract from the overwhelming sense of goodness, beauty, and truth that the pilgrim feels on first experiencing the church in person. Its flying buttresses, its stained glass, its great rose window with its delicate bar traceries that resemble the petals of the flowers, its richly carved portals, the soaring heights of its columns that flower into barrel vaults, its many shrines and reliquaries, its altars, and the presence of Jesus in the great tabernacle all work together to raise the pilgrim's mind to heavenly things.

Temko's description of just one of the front portals is enough to show how this house of God is intimately connected to the heavenly Jerusalem, peopled by the communion of angels and saints:

> Around the Virgin in majesty, in tiers of glory, is her Court of Heaven. Closest to her is a corps of fourteen angels; then fourteen patriarchs and sixteen prophets; and, outermost, sixteen old men of the Apocalypse, with their musical instruments and vials, as they were seen by St. John the Divine. . . . Singing, dancing, their rich beards tossing in the winds from the corner of the earth, they sail upward, as if mounted on a wheel of air, to the Lamb of God and, at the apex of the triangle, to the Christ of the Apocalypse — *alpha* and *omega*, the beginning and the end, the first and the last, whose terrible, two-bladed sword, after seven centuries, has shattered his teeth.[4]

In this cathedral, faith is incarnational, just as the Catholic Faith is an incarnational Faith — "the Word became flesh."[5] The kingdom of God is manifest to us, century after century, through the medium of this church building, stone laid upon stone, sculpture after sculpture hewn from rock, built and carved of human hands — a Gospel in stone brought to life!

But Temko doesn't stop there.

In the same breath, he describes the hundreds of gargoyles — inhuman bird-like figures with half-human faces — perched and grimacing on the balustrades overlooking the city. These grotesques were driven from the interior of the church by the Virgin, who banished them from her sanctuary but kept them as terrifying guardians of her outer walls and towers. This building, we easily understand, is a representation *in toto* of Christendom, from the saving power of Christ to the doom of the fallen and damned. The

---

[4] Temko, *Notre-Dame of Paris*, 189.

[5] John 1:14.

Notre Dame preaches the gospel in stone through its many works of sacred art, those beautifully crafted representations, both figural and symbolic, that point beyond themselves to religious truths.

Notre Dame is a permanent structure — massive and durable, meant to withstand the violence of man and the brutality of nature. For more than eight hundred years, the cathedral has stood as a survivor of many epochs, witnessing to the permanence of the gospel and of Christian society.

pilgrim senses here the spiritual struggle between good and evil, between the sacred and the profane, between the eternal and the temporal.

☞

Notre Dame Cathedral exemplifies
the best in church architecture

Notre Dame is easily recognized as art in the noblest sense, architecture of the highest order, a building established as a "sacred place" — a sacred place that is first of all, a house of God, a place of His earthly habitation, wrought in the fashion of heavenly things.

But what makes it so?

First, Notre Dame is a permanent structure — massive and durable, meant to withstand the violence of man and the brutality of nature. It has served as a silent witness to the tumultuous history of France over the past eight hundred years in the heart of its grand capital. It has stood as a survivor of many epochs, witnessing to the permanence of the Gospel and Christian society, despite the secularization of almost everything around the great cathedral. The edifice has transcended both time and culture — not an easy feat: it is a *permanent* structure.

Second, the heavenly and eternal is evoked through the soaring heights of the cathedral's interior spaces, made possible by the many elements of the Gothic structural system (pointed arches, flying buttresses, and vaulted ceilings, for instance). Thus, it is a *vertical* structure.

Third, the grand cathedral is "brought to life" as a gospel in stone through its many works of sacred art, those beautifully crafted representations, both figural and symbolic, that point well beyond themselves to religious truths. In other words, Notre Dame presents an *iconographic* architecture. The pilgrim can almost hear the patriarch Jacob, after his dream of angels ascending to and descending from Heaven, announcing, "How awesome is this place! This is none other than the house of God, and this is the gate of Heaven."[6]

☙

*Notre Dame Cathedral reveals
the natural laws of church architecture*

One basic tenet that architects have accepted for millennia is that the built environment has the capacity to affect the human person deeply — the way he acts, the way he feels, and the way he *is*. Church architects of past and present understood that the atmosphere created by the church building affects not only how we worship, but also what we believe. Ultimately, what we believe affects how we live our lives. It's difficult to separate theology and ecclesiology from the environment for worship, whether it's a traditional church or a modern church. If a Catholic church building doesn't reflect Catholic theology and ecclesiology, if the building undermines or dismisses the natural laws of church architecture, the worshiper risks accepting a Faith that is foreign to Catholicism.

Architecture isn't inconsequential.

That's why the Church's *Code of Canon Law* explicitly defines the church building as "a sacred building destined for divine worship." The *Catechism of the Catholic Church* reiterates this point and goes further by stating that "visible churches are not simply gathering places but signify and make visible the Church living in this place, the dwelling of God with men reconciled and united in Christ."[7]

This is a tall order, to be sure, and the architect today naturally wonders how a mere building can accomplish so much. Fortunately he doesn't stand alone in a perilous vacuum but has at his

[6] Gen. 28:17.
[7] *Catechism of the Catholic Church*, no. 1180.

*Notre Dame evokes the heavenly and the eternal through
the soaring heights of its interior spaces, made possible by the many
elements of the Gothic structural system. Thus, it's a vertical structure.*

Iconography is perhaps the most direct and efficacious way to achieve a transcendent architecture. The worthy church building presents an iconography that points to transcendent truths.

command more than fifteen hundred years of his craft on which to reflect.

When he turns to the Church's great architectural heritage, he discovers that from the Early Christian basilicas in Rome to the Gothic Revival churches of early twentieth-century America, the natural laws of church architecture are adhered to faithfully in the design of successful Catholic churches, buildings that serve both God and man as transcendental structures, transmitting eternal truths for generations to come. Indeed, it's remarkable that churches of every century — grand and small, in large cities, small towns, and rural settings — have achieved what Notre Dame has achieved through faithful adherence to these natural laws.

Yes, the results are manifested in individual styles, products of a particular time and place, each of which the Church has gladly admitted into her treasury of sacred architecture.[8] Yet each also serves as a house of God that looks to the past, serves the present, and informs the future.

How do they achieve this?

In every case, these successful church buildings firmly establish a sacred place to be used for worship of the triune God, both in private devotion and in public liturgy, and they make Christ's presence firmly known in their surroundings.

In every case, they conform to the three natural laws of verticality, permanence, and iconography, as exemplified in Notre Dame Cathedral.[9]

---

[8] "The Church . . . has welcomed those changes in materials, style, or ornamentation which the progress of the technical arts has brought with the passage of time. . . . The Church has not adopted any particular style of art as her very own": *Sacrosanctum Concilium* (Vatican II's Constitution on the Sacred Liturgy, 1963), no. 122, 123.

[9] The natural laws of verticality, permanence, and iconography are a loose translation — that is, specifically in reference to the architecture of the church edifice — of the ancient

Ugly as Sin

These natural laws are perhaps taken for granted by many, yet, for those who seek to understand how Catholic churches ought — and ought not — to be built, they're the most obvious starting points, primarily because these qualities create the proper atmosphere for worshiping God.

Consider the alternative: if Notre Dame lacked verticality, permanence, and iconography, Hugo wouldn't have written a novel about a hunchbacked bell-ringer, nor would Temko have composed what he calls a "biography" of the great cathedral. In fact, if it didn't adhere to the natural laws of church architecture, Notre Dame wouldn't exist today in any meaningful way. Lacking verticality, the cathedral wouldn't have inspired us toward the otherworldly; it wouldn't have effectively served as the soul of medieval Paris, let alone the present metropolis; nor would it have effectively marked Christ and His Church present and active in the French capital. Without permanence, the building would have been destroyed by barbarians or revolutionaries centuries ago. Devoid of iconography, Notre Dame would never have attracted pilgrims to this gospel in stone.

In other words, without the qualities of verticality, permanence, and iconography, Notre Dame wouldn't have established itself as a sacred place; it wouldn't be known to us today.

architect Vitruvius's three requirements for building: *utilitas, firmitas,* and *venustas* — "utility, strength, and beauty," or, translated by the architects of the Renaissance, "commodity, firmness, and delight." *Commodity* refers to the utility or usefulness of a building. In terms of sacred architecture, the utility (bringing the heavenly Jerusalem down to us) is represented by the verticality of the structure. In other words, the structure itself is a vertical sign pointing toward God. Permanence fulfills Vitruvius's requirement of *firmitas,* or "firmness," while "delight" (beauty) is accomplished in church architecture through the iconography, encompassing both form and artistic expression, of the structure.

The three natural laws of church architecture

Therefore, let's consider more closely each of these three natural laws, which are indispensable to successful Catholic church architecture.

☞

The first natural law:
A Catholic church must have verticality

In contrast to most other buildings, the successful church is so constructed that the vertical element dominates the horizontal. The soaring heights of its spaces speak to us of reaching toward Heaven, of transcendence — bringing the heavenly Jerusalem down to us through the medium of the church building. It's no coincidence that the text the Church reads in the Liturgy for the dedication of a church is taken from St. John's vision of the celestial Jerusalem:

> And I saw the holy city, New Jerusalem, coming down out of Heaven from God, made ready as a bride adorned for her husband. And I heard a loud voice from the throne saying, "Behold the dwelling of God with men, and He will dwell with them; and they will be His people, and God Himself will be with them as their God. And God will wipe away every tear from their eyes; and death shall be no more; neither shall there be mourning nor crying nor pain anymore, for the former things have passed away."[10]

According to these words of St. John, the interior spaces of the church ought to be characterized by a dramatic sense of height — in a word, verticality. It's a fact of human experience that verticality, the massing of volumes upward, most readily creates an atmosphere of transcendence and, in turn, enables man to create a building that expresses a sense of the spiritual and the heavenly.

[10] Rev. 21:2-4.

*Verticality — the massing of volumes upward — most readily creates
an atmosphere of transcendence and, in turn, enables man to create
a building that expresses a sense of the spiritual and the heavenly.
The church's architectural elements, such as windows, columns,
buttresses, and sacred art, should reinforce this heavenward aspiration.*

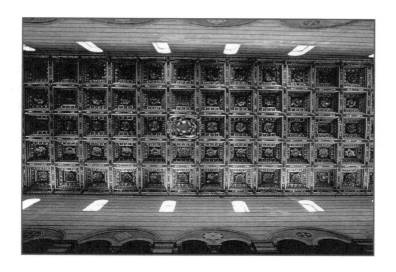

The articulation of the ceiling or dome creates a sense of reaching toward the heavenly Jerusalem through the use of mosaics, murals, and coffering, as well as by incorporating the mysterious play of light into the church's body.

Ugly as Sin

It's this transcendence that makes sacred architecture at all possible. The building's architectural elements — such as windows, columns, buttresses, and sacred art — should reinforce this heavenward aspiration. Likewise, the articulation of the ceiling should further create a sense of reaching toward the heavenly Jerusalem through the use of mosaics, murals, and coffering, as well as by incorporating the mysterious play of natural light into the body of the church.

Consider also that the early Christians, prior to the Constantinian era, solemnized the Holy Sacrifice of the Mass in inconspicuous places — most likely in homes and sometimes in the catacombs — that had no recourse to an emphasized verticality. Yet once public Christian worship was legalized by Constantine, the Christians quickly adopted the basilica form, in which spaces were emphatically vertical and conspicuous. Not only did the soaring spaces of such structures lend themselves to symbolizing the reaching toward God and toward things heavenly; it also represented a kingly nobility, for the basilica was the Roman "House of the King," fittingly adapted as the House of the King of Kings.

It's difficult, isn't it, to visualize the kind of spaces that would be created if the ceilings in such grand churches as Notre Dame, St. Peter's Basilica, or Constantinople's Hagia Sophia were lowered to, say, twelve feet or even thirty feet. Despite the exemplary iconography and permanence of these structures, they would fall drastically short as sacred places, as houses of God, if their building's proportions were reduced to reflect an emphasis on the horizontal rather than on the vertical.

This need to emphasize the reaching toward the heavens was primarily what inspired Gothic builders to develop a structural system that allowed for even greater soaring spaces. The Gothic architect knew that without an emphasized verticality, the church is effectively emasculated, its *raison d'être* subverted.

⌒

The second natural law:
A Catholic church must have permanence

The church building, representing Christ's presence in a particular place, is also necessarily a permanent structure ("Christ is the same yesterday and today and forever"[11]) conceived in theory and practice "with a firm foundation." So, too, is the Catholic Church enduring and permanent, transcending space and time. The medieval canonist Bishop Gulielmus Durandus (1220-1296) reminds us that the Church is built with all strength, "upon the foundations of the apostles and prophets, Jesus Christ Himself being the chief cornerstone. Her foundations are in the holy mountains."[12] The permanence of our church structures reflects these qualities of the universal Church. And just as verticality points to the heavenly and the eternal, so, too, does the requisite principle of permanence. It's another way in which architects create an atmosphere of transcendence.

Nineteenth-century architect Eugène Emmanuel Viollet-le-Duc writes of Notre Dame that "everyone who understands construction will be amazed when he sees what numberless precautions are resorted to in the execution — how the prudence of the practical builder is combined with the daring of the artist full of power and inventive imagination."[13] Viollet-le-Duc refers to the permanence of what has become known to us as the Gothic structural system, an ingenious method of building that lends itself both to verticality — soaring heights enabled by the unique system of buttressing — and permanence. The Gothic churches constructed in

[11] Heb. 13:8.

[12] Gulielmus Durandus, *Rationale Divinorum Officiorum*. Durandus's treatise is regarded as the standard source on Liturgy in the thirteenth century.

[13] Eugène Emmanuel Viollet-le-Duc, "Construction," *Dictionary of French Architecture, 1854-68*.

*Churches such as the Florence Cathedral were
conceived as solid, enduring temples, perpetual
reminders of Christ's presence active in the world.*

Europe throughout the medieval centuries can't be accused of being cheap, tawdry structures doomed to decay. No, structures such as Notre Dame were conceived as solid and enduring temples, perpetual reminders of Christ's presence active in the world. The same can be said of most churches built in the Early Christian, Romanesque, Byzantine, Renaissance, Baroque, and Neoclassical styles. Each of these architectural epochs has respected the necessity of permanence.

There are several ways a church can assert its permanence. First, and most obvious, is by its durability. The church, a building that will serve generation after generation, transcending time and culture, must be constructed of durable materials. Mere sticks and stones, shingles and tar won't do. Typically, one or another type of masonry construction is used, employing the finest materials available.

Related to durability is massing: the church must be of significant mass, built with solid foundations, thick walls, and allowing for generous interior spaces. This massing is another aspect of the architectural language of churches. It's integral to both verticality (the massing of volumes upward creates verticality) and iconography (the massing of the church helps it convey its iconic meaning, i.e., its massing can make the church look like a church and function like a church).

Third is continuity. Churches whose design grows organically out of the past two millennia of churches identify themselves with the life of the Church throughout those two millennia and, by their continuity with the history and tradition of Catholic church architecture, manifest in another way the permanence of the Faith.

In other words, to convey that aspect of permanence rooted in continuity, the architectural language of churches must develop *organically* throughout time, such as when the language of the Renaissance churches permutated into the Baroque language, or when the Gothic forms emerged from the language of the Romanesque.

Early Christian

Romanesque

Byzantine

Gothic

Continuity: The authentic Catholic church building is a work of art that
acknowledges the previous greatness of the Church's architectural patrimony.
It refers to the past, serves the present, and informs the future.

Renaissance

Baroque

Neoclassical

Neogothic

In both cases, the growth of the language was organic. The style may have changed, as when the semicircular arch gave way to the pointed arch. But here was no sudden break with tradition, no disregard for the churches of past centuries (arches were as much a part of the Gothic language as the Romanesque). Architects built on what they knew from the past, refining certain aspects of the language and developing others.

Architects of future generations need to comprehend the language of church architecture in order to build permanent sacred edifices for their own times and future centuries. No successful church architect can be — or even pretend to be — ignorant of the Church's historical patrimony. Continuity demands that a successful church design can't spring from the whims of man or the fashion of the day. The architect who breaks completely with architectural tradition robs his church of the quality of permanence that is essential to any successful church design. An authentic Catholic church building is a work of art that acknowledges the previous greatness of the Church's architectural patrimony: it refers to the past, serves the present, and informs the future.

⌒

The third natural law:
A Catholic church must have iconography

The third requisite principle is that of iconography, which speaks specifically to the "sign" value of the building. First, the structure itself ought to be an icon. This is accomplished primarily through its form and the church's relation to the surrounding environment, whether urban or rural. Second, the worthy church building presents an iconography that points to something other than itself. St. Thomas Aquinas,[14] among other great intellectuals

---

[14] St. Thomas Aquinas (c. 1225-1274), Dominican philosopher, theologian, and Doctor of the Church.

who preceded him by centuries, realized that man's mind is raised to contemplation through material objects. Likewise, in his *Spiritual Exercises*, published in 1548, St. Ignatius Loyola[15] stressed the importance of visualizing the subjects of meditation; painting, sculpture, and architecture are meant to work together to produce a unified effect.

Thus, it's here that these works of art,[16] the material objects that are effective to this end, with their reliance on the breadth of religious symbolism, come into play. Architectural beauty should reflect God's creation, particularly man, who is created in the image and likeness of God. It should beget an environment that lifts man's soul from secular things and brings it into harmony with the heavenly.

Architect Ralph Adams Cram wrote, "Art has been, is, and will be forever, the greatest agency for spiritual impression that the Church may claim."[17] It's for this reason, he adds, that art is in its highest manifestation the expression of religious truths. It's through art that Christians have developed the ingenious symbolism that raises our faculties of soul to God. The tradition of iconography and symbolism in Catholic culture is broad and rich. Meaning is conveyed through formal elements, from basic geometric shapes[18]

---

[15] St. Ignatius Loyola (1491-1556), founder of the Jesuit Order.

[16] It's universally understood that true art is that which evokes an experience that will be aesthetic, emotional, and intellectual, reflecting the three transcendentals of goodness, beauty, and truth. It's universally understood that religious art not only points to something greater than itself, but effects meditation and contemplation of that something, which will most likely be some religious truth, e.g., the Incarnation, the Holy Trinity, or the cardinal virtues.

[17] Ralph Adams Cram, *Church Building* (Boston: Marshall Jones Co., 1899), 9.

[18] Such as the triangle that symbolizes the Holy Trinity or the four interlocking circles that represent the four evangelists.

to figural imagery[19] to literal representation of people or scenes, as in sculpture or paintings. The meanings conveyed through a church's iconographic programs are most typically that of religious truths or historical events of religious significance. They're always expressions of the Catholic Faith.

Inspired by churchmen such as St. Ignatius and St. Charles Borromeo,[20] the masters of the Catholic Counter Reformation, for instance, expressed the Catholic Faith in the very birth of their art by means of elaborate high altars and tabernacles, special niche and aisle shrines dedicated to the Virgin Mary and to the saints, prominent pulpits for preaching, and an abundance of art in glass, sculpture, mosaic, and painting devised to teach the truths necessary for salvation. The atmosphere created on this model is one of religious mystery wherein we can experience a little of the unearthly joy of the New Jerusalem, where we can encounter Christ in a unique way. These iconographic churches, these icons, tell the story of Christ and His Church; they teach, catechize, and illustrate the lives of the Church's saintly souls. They manifest eternal and transcendental truths.

Again, if we're to look to Notre Dame, we understand easily how a pilgrim can spend days — even weeks — meditating on the mysteries that are "enfleshed" in the architecture of the cathedral's sculptural programs. A student of the Church may spend months and years reflecting on the ingenuity and beauty of the Catholic truths revealed in the art and architecture of this gospel in stone. Ordinary laymen, too, are drawn into the church, into the house of God, attracted by the iconography of this medieval edifice, which still speaks clearly to us today, more than eight hundred years later.

---

[19] Such as the lion that represents St. Mark or the lily that symbolizes the Immaculate Conception.

[20] St. Charles Borromeo (1538-1584), Archbishop of Milan.

The three natural laws of church architecture

This is possible only because architecture has the capacity to carry meaning. A church building is a "vessel of meaning" with the greatest of symbolic responsibilities: it must bear the significance of eternal truths that are transmitted through its material form, its adorning architectural elements, and its sacred works of art. These elements — indeed the whole of the church edifice — must create an other-worldly feel that inspires man to worship God, to humble himself before his Creator, to partake in the sacred mysteries, and to focus himself on the eternal. Iconography is yet another way — perhaps the most direct and efficacious way — to achieve a transcendent architecture.

These three natural laws of church architecture — verticality, permanence, and iconography — transcend the different epochs of Christianity, which is why they're qualities of all the truly great churches of Christendom. They're the foundation, as it were, on which good church architects build churches that succeed in becoming for their own time and for all generations gates of Heaven and worthy houses of God.

Chapter Two

⌒

Our pilgrim goes into the house of the Lord
(or, the essential elements of every proper church)

Architects who build successful Catholic churches rely on the three natural laws of church architecture, but, over the centuries, have developed many other ways by which they employ elements of the church structure as means to draw souls to God and to teach them about the Faith and help awaken in them the responses of awe and reverence that are called for by the encounter with God Himself in His dwelling.

One of the best ways to learn about these architectural elements is to travel with a pilgrim as he makes his way to a Catholic church, enters it, and moves forward through the church to the sanctuary.

Let's send our pilgrim first to a traditional Catholic church and watch with him as he encounters it from afar and up close. Let's consider the experience that the church affords him and what that says about God and our pilgrim's relation to God. Then let's have that same pilgrim approach a modern Catholic church in the same way, enter it, and move toward the tabernacle there. Then we'll evaluate the experience that the modern Church affords him.

By this method, we'll be able to gauge the success of each church as an appropriate house of God and as an architectural instrument meant to serve the faithful and manifest the Faith.

Ugly as Sin

Our pilgrim approaches a traditional church. From the time he catches a glimpse of that bell tower, steeple, or dome in the distance to the moment he approaches the altar of God to receive the Holy Sacrament, he is, in the traditional sense, making a pilgrimage. He's seeking the heavenly Kingdom; he's seeking God, and he desires the salvation God offers us through the eternal sacrifice of His Son.

This experience is accomplished in the eucharistic celebration of the Paschal mystery, in which Christ is "at the summit of the revelation of the inscrutable mystery of God."[21] We undertake this pilgrimage in imitation of our forefathers in Faith who ascended the Holy Mountain at Jerusalem for the great solemnities of Passover, the Feast of Weeks, and the Feast of Tabernacles. The tribes of Israel journeyed forth from neighboring villages and distant cities to praise the name of the Lord, to enter into communion with Him in worship while dwelling in the tent of His sanctuary.

It was also in Jerusalem that the central event in the history of salvation took place: Christ's Paschal mystery.[22] Thus, it's no coincidence that the Holy Land was the first sacred place of devotional pilgrimage both for the Hebrews, who had been led by Moses into that Promised Land flowing with milk and honey, and

---

[21] Pope John Paul II, *Dives in misericordia,* no. 8.

[22] "Jesus' road does not end on the hill called Golgotha. The earthly pilgrimage of Christ crosses the boundary of death, into the infinite and in the mystery of God, beyond death. On the mount of the Ascension, the final step of His pilgrimage takes place. As He promises to come back, the risen Lord rises to Heaven and goes to His Father's house to prepare a place for us, so that where He is, we may be with Him, too. In fact, this is how He summarizes His mission: 'I came from the Father and have come into the world and now I leave the world to go to the Father. . . . Father, I want those You have given me to be with me where I am, so that they may always see the glory You have given me' ": "The Pilgrimage in the Great Jubilee," paragraph 10, Pontifical Council for the Care of Migrants and Itinerant People, 1999.

for Christians, who have never ceased honoring the holy places of the birth, life, death, and Resurrection of Jesus Christ and those that marked the beginnings of the Church.

In our own pilgrimages today — to our parish church, to the local cathedral, to Lourdes, to Rome, to the Holy Land — we honor the heavenly Jerusalem, which is replicated on earth through the consecration of each church. This "new Jerusalem," built of material goods by the hands of men, isn't a mere representation of the Holy Land of the Middle East, but is a portent of the heavenly kingdom and a reminder of our eternal pilgrimage to our Father's house. Our pilgrimage, therefore, has a transcendent end in which we're destined to be "citizens with the saints, and members of the household of God."[23]

The church building, reflecting the Church herself, should assist us in this eternal pilgrimage by drawing us near, serving as our maternal sanctuary, facilitating the Church's Liturgy,[24] and memorializing the Holy Sacrifice on Calvary. With this in mind, let's consider the various parts of the church building as a sequence of spaces and furnishings that work together in service of our great pilgrimage to our Father's house.

☞

A traditional church beckons to souls from afar

During His Sermon on the Mount, Jesus taught His followers that they were to be the light of the world. "A city set on a hill cannot be hid," He said, just as men do not "light a lamp and put it under a bushel, but on a stand, and it gives light to all in the

---

[23] Eph. 2:19.

[24] Another expression of pilgrimage is the liturgical procession, e.g., the Corpus Christi procession, the procession of palms on Palm Sunday, or the veneration of the Cross on Good Friday. Our churches are sacred places that accommodate and encourage the pilgrimage in its many forms.

During His Sermon on the Mount, Jesus taught His followers that
they were to be the light of the world: "A city set on a hill cannot be hid."
In terms of churches, the words of Christ are instructive. Suitably,
another historical term for the church building is a "city on a hill."

house."[25] For church architects, the words of Christ are instructive. As we have already seen, our houses of God need to show Christ and His Church present and active in a particular locale. Suitably, another historical term for the church building is a "city on a hill." This refers not only to the preferred location of our churches in high places (just as Solomon's Temple was built on Mount Moriah, the highest point in Jerusalem), with the sense of being a fortified, protected sanctuary, but also as occupying a place of prominence in the community. The church building shouldn't be hidden, because hidden signs are bad signs ("a city on a hill cannot be hid"). Rather, the church should be integrated into the neighborhood and landscape so that its location reminds the pilgrim of the building's importance and purpose.

When that's done, there's no doubt that the church is the most important structure in the environment. By the church's physical location, the pilgrim recognizes that Christ is, was, and will be "present and active" in this locale.

Not only does a church serve as a beacon by its situation on the heights or its rising high above the cornfields, but it's audible, too. Through its bells, the pilgrim is reminded of Christ's presence, His importance in the lives of the faithful, and our need to honor Him in adoration and prayer. All tolls and peals of the church bells, no matter what the occasion or time of day, are a summons to prayer — whether for the souls of the faithful departed, for the pious recitation of the *Angelus*, or as a call to worship through participation in the Holy Sacrifice of the Mass.

The pilgrim can't help but be profoundly moved by the peal of cathedral bells, by the ebullient ringing of wedding bells, or by the mournful toll of the funeral bell. For our pilgrim, that distant sound may well be the first indication that his destination isn't far off. He then looks forward to catching his first glimpse of the

[25] Cf. Matt. 5:14.

church tower or spire rising above the urban fabric or seeing the silhouette of the church building atop a distant hill.

The bell tower, often called the *campanile*, is one of the primary elements that draws the pilgrim to the church from a great distance, not only by the sound of its bells, but by its visual profile. Pointing upward to the heavens, it's a welcoming sign to pilgrims and tourists, parishioners and merchants alike.

In other church buildings, the dome, rather than the campanile, is the primary ascendant element, especially in those Renaissance and Renaissance-inspired churches that are so familiar to

The typical Venetian campanile, such as this one at San Giorgio Church, is built as a tall, slim, square shaft that's frequently tapered, rising to an open belfry. This Venetian-style campanile was revived during the nineteenth century in England and in North America.

In some churches, the dome is the primary ascendant element,
especially in those Renaissance and Renaissance-inspired
churches that are so familiar to the pilgrim.

*The dome also has significant effects on the interior:
it adds to the sense of verticality and transcendence —
symbolizing the heavenly kingdom — of the church in
its height and in the way shafts of light
penetrate the church's interior.*

our pilgrim. Unlike the campanile, the dome has significant effects on the interior of the church: it adds to the verticality and sense of transcendence — symbolizing the heavenly kingdom — in both its height and in the way it allows shafts of light to penetrate the interior of the church.

⁀

The traditional church's atrium leads us
from the profane to the sacred

As our pilgrim makes his way from the vanity and materialism of the world toward the sacred womb of God's sanctuary, guided by pealing bells and the compass of tower, dome, or steeple, the connection between the church and its surroundings becomes important. This juncture has been successfully addressed for centuries in urban areas through the *piazza* (plaza or square). Here's a place for the faithful to congregate, for the curious to linger and gaze upon the church; it's the first transitional space that prepares us for our dramatic entrance into the gate of Heaven, and it's a place that often serves as a backdrop for functions both religious and civic.

On a much smaller scale than the piazza is the *atrium,* an open courtyard (recalling the forecourts of Solomon's Temple) that's more of an integrated element of the church building.[26] In the center of the atrium, which is surrounded by colonnades of a cloister, is a fountain, where our pilgrim washes his hands before entering the church. Flowers and greenery give the effect of a garden. As such, the atrium is otherwise referred to as a *paradisus,* having obvious biblical connotations, not the least of which is the Garden of Eden, where our first parents lived in innocence before the

---

[26] In his manifesto that inspired the architecture of Counter Reformation churches, especially in Italy, St. Charles Borromeo recommended that wherever there is space, and funds permit, an atrium should be built in front of the church, surrounded by cloisters with columns.

Ugly as Sin

day of the serpent. The symbolism of the atrium as paradise is rich: just as the garden in Genesis was the earthly forecourt to the heavenly kingdom, so the atrium serves as the forecourt to the house of God. And those who stand at the forecourt, as did Adam and Eve, can choose the profanity of the world by following the serpent or the sacredness of the *porta coeli* by approaching the altar of God.

The piazza hearkens back to the Greek agora ("open space"), the center of political, commercial, religious, and social life in the cities of ancient Greece. The agora, surrounded by public buildings and temples, frequently with colonnades on the side facing the square, gives precedent to the piazzas of Italy, which often use the colonnades of buildings to mark their perimeters. In turn, the piazzas of Italy, such as Piazza San Marco in Venice, gave rise to the "Cathedral squares" of northern and eastern Europe and North America.

*Flowers and greenery give the effect of a garden. As such,
the atrium, such as this one at Rome's St. Paul Outside
the Walls, is referred to as a* paradisus, *having obvious
biblical connotations, particularly the Garden of Eden.*

Such atriums have been a part of churches since the early
Christian ones, such as Old St. Peter's in Rome and Hagia Sophia
in Constantinople. At the "new" Basilica of St. Peter, Gianlorenzo Bernini integrated atrium and piazza to produce Christendom's most recognizable colonnaded forecourt: St. Peter's Square
(1667). This dynamic ovular space, formed by two vast semicircular colonnades, designed to accommodate major liturgical events,
is richly symbolic. According to Bernini himself, the form of the
colonnade that encloses the large piazza was designed "to receive
in a maternal gesture Catholics in order to confirm their belief,

At the "new" Basilica of St. Peter, Gianlorenzo Bernini
integrated atrium and piazza to produce Christendom's
most recognizable colonnaded forecourt: St. Peter's Square.

heretics in order to reunite them with the Church, and infidels in order to reveal to them the true Faith."[27]

The familiar colonnade appears as the extended arms of Holy Mother Church, welcoming the faithful with a huge embrace. This metaphor is farther reaching than it first appears. The church building, reflecting the Church herself, is maternal — the womb, so to speak, that serves both as sanctuary to the faithful and as home to God in a very real and particular way.

[27] Christian Norberg-Schulz, *Baroque Architecture* (New York: Rizzoli International Publications, 1986), 27.

Alas, not all churches can accommodate a proper atrium. When having an open courtyard isn't possible, some churches have instead a large porch, or *portico*. These covered exterior spaces serve useful liturgical purposes, as does the atrium — for instance, at the beginning of the processions on Palm Sunday and at the Easter Vigil. From ancient times, the Easter Vigil has been considered the pre-eminent event in the Church's liturgical cycle. Since the restoration of the rites of Holy Week by order of Pope Pius XII, the Vigil has assumed its former grandeur and primacy of place. It's here in the atrium or on the porch in the darkness of Holy Saturday night that the Easter fire is kindled and the Easter candle blessed with the Church's beautiful ritual, full of symbolism and Christological meaning. After the candle is lit from the fire, a procession forms as the candle is held aloft, with the faithful bearing small candles lit from the flame of the Easter candle. Then all enter into the darkened church, chanting *lumen Christi*, "light of Christ." It's this light of Christ that the church ought to broadcast in every element of its building, as well as through the unity of its parts as a whole.

⌐

The traditional church's façade tells us
of the riches awaiting us inside

Once the pilgrim draws near to the church building, standing perhaps in the piazza or near the fountain of the arcade-studded atrium, he comes face-to-face with the *façade*, that is, the front exterior. Often the most memorable part of the building, the façade may incorporate a bell tower or other towers, statuary, sculptural reliefs, frescoes, stained-glass windows, and, of course, the main entrance doors to the church. In a modern urban setting, in which a church (such as St. Patrick's Cathedral in New York City) may be dwarfed by surrounding structures, the façade takes on an extra importance in that the church itself becomes identified with its façade. This front entrance is the "face" that the church presents to the world. It's often the only part of the building that people will see (not everyone enters the house of God, unfortunately), and thus it's the façade that has the greatest opportunity to evangelize, teach, and catechize. This is accomplished most obviously through the incorporation of exterior artwork.

The façades of the great churches of Christendom have been approached with great care by the architects of every age. History books show us that there's no one way to design the façade of a church. The emotionally elaborate Gothic exteriors, the austere, geometric-style "wall architecture" of the Renaissance, and the irregular, undulating sculptural façades of the Baroque all evoke a profound sense of goodness, beauty, and truth — that which naturally draws both the pious pilgrim and the curious skeptic nearer the *porta coeli*. All do so through very different means, yet it's an iconographic beauty that is at the basis of their creation: proper proportions, purity of forms, and manifold works of art.

The façade acts as a "vessel of meaning" in the most straightforward of ways: it's the foreword of a book as much as it's a grand *summa* — a foreword to the Catholic Liturgy that takes place inside, a prelude to the great truths of the Faith, and a welcoming invitation to the maternal sanctuary; simultaneously, it's a summary of the Faith in its totality (its catholicity).

Even the façades of some early basilica churches, often mistakenly described as "plain," were richly designed to fulfill their calling as vessels of meaning. The upper surfaces above the projecting portico were often ornamented with colorful mosaics. The major basilicas of Rome serve as excellent examples. They're perhaps the earliest evidence of façades that are meant to inspire, awe, and invite, while "telling a story." Yet while the façades of the churches of the first millennium were indeed beautiful vessels of meaning, none compared with the Gothic façades of later centuries in complexity, detail, and craftsmanship. Victor Hugo, for instance,

The front façade is the "face" that the church presents to the world. It's often the only part of the building that people see, and thus it has the greatest opportunity to evangelize, teach, and catechize. This is accomplished most obviously through the incorporation of exterior artwork.

makes this observation about the grand façade of the Parisian Notre Dame: ". . . crowding upward before the eye without disorder, their innumerable details of statuary, sculpture, and carving [create] a vast symphony in stone . . . like divine creation whose two-fold character it seems to have appropriated: variety, eternity." At Notre Dame, the pilgrim, standing at a distance in the cathedral square or on the steps of the cathedral, stands face-to-face with eternity — a feeling evoked by an architecture that evinces the natural laws of verticality, permanence, and iconography.

Two elements of the façade are of particular interest to our pilgrim: the front portals and the rose window. If only for practical purposes, the portal,[28] made up of the architectural elements surrounding the door, is of greatest importance in the façade. For this is the door to the *domus Dei*, to the *porta coeli*. It's the means through which our pilgrim reaches the threshold of God's house. Through the centuries, architects and church artists have responded to the obvious by paying particularly close attention to the design of the elements that surround the openings into the church. These are often elaborately treated with carved ornaments of saints, kings, men, animals, or foliage, depending on the popular symbols and images employed during different ages.

Our pilgrim recognizes biblical scenes from the Old Testament and from the life of Christ depicted in the semicircular arch above the deeply recessed central portal on what is called the tympanum. Since our pilgrim must enter the church through its doors, the space directly above each entrance provides the most prominent location for iconographic sculpture that serves as a visual extension to religious teaching. Accordingly, the portal sculpture is rich in both figural meaning and Christian symbolism.

Above the central portal is a large circular rose window of awe-inspiring beauty. Our pilgrim likens the segments of stained glass

---

[28] *Portal* is derived from the medieval Latin word for "city gate."

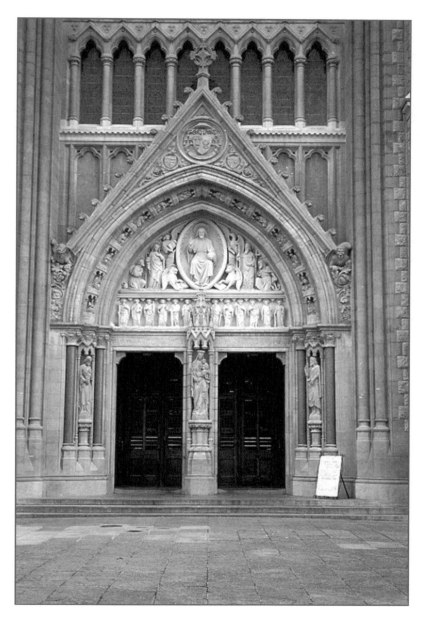

The portal is of greatest importance in the façade,
for the portal is the door to the domus Dei, *to the* porta coeli.

The tympanum scene of the Last Judgment was perhaps the most common New Testament narrative depicted during the twelfth century. One of the most vivid of these, with angels and demons portrayed, is Chartres Cathedral's famous Portail Royal (1155), part of the only remaining element from the Romanesque church that burned to the ground in 1194.

that radiate from its center to the unfolding petals of a rose. The rose isn't only one of the most beautiful flowers of God's creation, but it's also our Lady's most prolific emblem. Representing the beauty and love of the Virgin Mary, this rose is at the heart of the façade. At the center of this heart is an image of Christ sitting on the lap of the Virgin, who offers her incarnate Son to the world. The images that radiate from Christ are narrative images from Scripture and from the lives of the saints. Sometimes referred to as

The great rose window, American historian Henry Adams wrote, "is one of the flowers of architecture which reveals its beauties slowly without end."

"the eye of God," the rose window is a powerful work of art that anticipates the Beatific Vision of God's beauty in the eternal kingdom. It's a representation of the perfection, balance, and harmony of the purified soul as it prepares to enter that kingdom forever.

The traditional church's narthex draws us toward the sanctuary

When our pilgrim finally steps through the church doors, he has arrived. It's here in the narthex, the threshold of God's house, that he will pause to get his bearings, knock the snow from his boots, remove his hat, or close his umbrella. But this is no mere foyer, mudroom, or lobby; it's primarily the final transitional space from the outside world (the profane and temporal) to the church's interior (the sacred and eternal). It's here where our pilgrim will first smell lingering incense and the burning wax of vigil candles. It's here where he'll be given a hint of where he's headed. Thus, it's a dimly lit place decorated modestly with religious art, perhaps a crucifix hanging on the wall, with a prie-dieu beneath it. It's the first devotional space of God's house.

In addition to its primary function as a transitional space, the narthex serves a practical liturgical function: providing a place for processions to assemble. Thus, the narthex is known as the "galilee," since the procession from narthex to altar symbolizes Christ's journey from Galilee to Jerusalem for the Crucifixion. It isn't uncommon to see a wide red carpet beneath the central door to the nave leading down the central aisle up to the altar, a reminder of the symbolic road our Savior walked to redeem the world.

The traditional church's baptistery reminds us
of our entrance into the Church Universal

At one end of the narthex, our pilgrim passes the baptistery. He's reminded that he's a pilgrim also by reason that he has been baptized. Through this first sacrament of initiation, our pilgrim was not only reborn as an adopted son of God and sanctified as a temple of the Holy Spirit, but he was also incorporated into Christ and His Church through participation in Christ's death and Resurrection.[29] He becomes part of the "pilgrim Church on earth." It's fitting, then, that the catechumen pilgrim[30] be baptized at the threshold of God's house, here at the narthex.

The baptistery appears as a chapel, at the north end of the narthex (because pagans came predominately from the north). Polygonal in shape, the chapel contains a font consecrated for the sole purpose of Baptism, placed at the center beneath a cupola. The form of the chapel recalls that of the martyrium (a martyr shrine), thought to be most suitable because Baptism is equated with the descent into Christ's tomb and a rebirth into Christ's Resurrection, according to St. Paul's letter to the Romans: "You have died to the law through the body of Christ, so that you may belong to another, to Him who has been raised from the dead in order that we may bear fruit."[31]

The polygonal chapel often has eight sides, referring to the Resurrection as the "eighth day" (Sunday comes after Saturday, the Sabbath, or seventh day of the week).

The baptistery's location is also used to explain and symbolize the meaning of the sacrament. The location in the narthex, at the threshold of the church, is symbolic of the pilgrim's entrance into the Church universal. The spiritual rebirth, provided by the sacrament, fittingly takes place at this threshold of God's house. In

---

[29] "Do you not know that all of us who have been baptized into Christ Jesus were baptized into His death? We were buried therefore with Him by baptism into death, so that as Christ was raised from the dead by the glory of the Father, we too might walk in newness of life" (Rom. 6:3-4).

[30] A person preparing to be received into the Catholic Church.

[31] Rom. 7:4.

other words, just as Baptism is the beginning of a Catholic's pilgrimage to his heavenly Father as part of the pilgrim Church on earth, the baptistery is suitably placed at the threshold to God's house.

Our pilgrim understands readily that the font is the most significant part of the baptistery.[32] It's an iconographic element just as much as the baptistery itself. Designed and built as a beautiful piece of religious artwork, the font has Christian symbols and imagery sculpted into its pedestal and basin. The imagery depicts the struggle between good and evil: angels and devils battle for souls, and there are representations of snakes, dragons, and other beasts. Nevertheless, the most prominent image is that of St. John the Baptist, clad in a garment of camel hair tied with a leather girdle, and the Holy Spirit depicted as the descending dove, alluding to the Baptism of Jesus in the Jordan, "Behold, the heavens were opened and He saw the Spirit of God descending like a dove."[33]

The traditional church's nave declares that
the Church is the ark of salvation

Once through the narthex doors, our pilgrim finds himself in the main body of the church. As his eyes adjust to the relatively dim light at the back of the nave, he instinctively looks for the nearest holy water stoup into which he will dip his fingers to bless himself with the Sign of the Cross. The holy water reminds him of

[32] The baptismal font is depicted in early Christian art as a shallow basin in which the baptized stood with feet immersed, while water was poured over him from a vase held by a priest. Consequently, the early fonts, enshrined in the large baptistery buildings, were designed as shallow basins, recessed in the floor to receive the standing neophyte. Later, however, when infant Baptism became the norm, fonts were placed on pedestals over which the infant was held.

[33] Matt. 3:16.

his own baptism, when he was blessed with holy water and baptized into the mystery of the Holy Trinity. Each time he dips his hand into holy water, he recalls that through this sacrament he was made a child of God. Consequently he's reminded of his responsibility to keep God's commandments — to know, to love, and to serve God.

Holy water also reminds our pilgrim to be sorry for his sins, since blessings with holy water cleanse us of our venial sins. In fact, during some Masses, there's a rite of sprinkling. The priest or bishop walks down the aisle and blesses the congregation by sprinkling holy water over them. During this rite the *Asperges* is sung.[34]

The third reason our pilgrim uses holy water is for exorcism. An exorcism is literally driving away the Devil. The traditional prayer for the blessing of holy water emphasizes the power of holy water to exorcise:

> O God, Creator of unconquered power, King of invincible empire and Victor ever great: who put down the powers of hostile dominion and conquer the fury of the roaring enemy, who fight powerfully against our wicked foes: trembling we beseech You, O Lord, we implore You and beg You that You might graciously look upon this creature of water and salt, kindly illumine it, sanctify it with the dew of Your loving kindness, so that wherever it is sprinkled, through the invocation of Your holy Name, every infestation of the unclean spirit be cast out, and the terror of the poisonous serpent be driven far away. And may the presence of the Holy Spirit deign to be with us always, we who implore Your mercy.

[34] *Asperges* is Latin for "you will sprinkle," taken from Psalm 51: "You will sprinkle me with hyssop and I shall be cleansed: You will wash me, and I will be made whiter than snow."

Thus, when our pilgrim blesses himself with holy water, he's exorcising himself. He's protecting himself from "the fury of the roaring enemy." All of this considered, then, it is right and just that our pilgrim purifies himself with holy water on entering fully into God's house, into this first wholly sacred place. He does this by making the Sign of the Cross, the outward gesture that reminds him of the Holy Trinity: Father, Son, and Holy Spirit.

Once our pilgrim's eyes adjust, he finds himself both awed and humbled by the cavernous space commonly called the *nave*, a term derived from the Latin word for "ship" (from which we get the English word *naval*). This is the place where the worshiping congregation dwells and is called *nave* because it represents the "ark of salvation." The symbolism of the boat, ship, or the ark is rich in both Scripture and Tradition. A boat signifies safety and well-being, usually during a tumultuous voyage. Noah's protection from the flood via the ark designed to God's specifications is the most obvious allusion. But the Church herself is this ark, too, sometimes referred to as the Barque of Peter, the place where Christians are given sanctuary and are guided on their pilgrimage to the Father's house. We see this represented in Scripture when the apostles encounter a fierce storm while crossing the Sea of Galilee. They're convinced that their death is inescapable, yet Jesus, when awakened from His slumber, assures them of their safety and chides them for their lack of faith in Him.[35]

In the same way, the nave is also symbolic of the mother's womb, in which pilgrims are kept in a nurturing environment that helps them to develop, mature, and grow toward their eternal destination with God in the heavenly kingdom. The Church, in fact, has long been referred to as *Mater Ecclesia*, Mother Church, mother of all. The church building, then, is a physical representation of the maternal place on earth, where the pilgrim goes so as

[35] Cf. Mark 4:36-40.

The nave's central processional aisle leads directly to the sanctuary and the altar, where the Church memorializes and re-presents in an unbloody manner Christ's one, holy Sacrifice on the Cross.

no longer to feel a foreigner, where he goes for sanctuary. It's a sacred place conducive to prayer and worship.

The Fathers of the Church often spoke of the maternity of the Church, and church builders have long manifested this maternal aspect of the Church in her sacred structures. Thus, the church building is also seen as a representation of Mary, who nurtured in her womb and brought forth the incarnate Son. This was reflected particularly in the Middle Ages, when almost all of the Gothic cathedrals in France were named after Our Lady: *Notre Dame*. This maternal aspect also accounts for the significance of Marian imagery and symbols in churches, most of which represent her as the Mother of Jesus, the Mother of God, or as Mother of the Church, the Mother of All. In this way, we can see that Mary, too, leads our pilgrim to Christ, helps him remain "on the Way," in the safety of the Barque of Peter.

Another aspect of the nave is that it's always directed toward the sanctuary, at the head of the building. Indeed the nave is also a representation of the body at the service of the head, just as the Body of Christ is at the service of Christ the Head. A famous diagram shows the image of Christ superimposed over a floor plan of a typical basilica-style church, and this is informative. The head of Christ fits in the sanctuary; the arms become the transepts, and the torso and legs fill out the nave. So here we can see literally the idea of the church building representing the body of Christ. Neither is it a coincidence that the floor plan is laid out in the shape of a cross, called cruciform, which reminds us of Christ on the Cross.

The traditional church's pews promote
adoration, directing our eyes to the altar

Just as the "ark of salvation" is prepared to receive our pilgrim, the nave is also prepared to serve the public liturgy of the Church. The layout and various artistic and architectural elements that the nave comprises help to reflect Christ's journey from Galilee to Jerusalem, that same journey that plays out during the Mass. Here, our pilgrim easily comprehends that the nave is divided into four sections of seating with a central processional aisle leading to the sanctuary and altar, where the Church memorializes and re-presents in an unbloody manner Christ's one holy Sacrifice on the Cross. Two side aisles, one on each side of the processional aisle, also lead to the sanctuary up front.

*Perhaps the most common elements of the nave are
the pews and their kneelers. The traditional arrangement
of the pews is unidirectional, facing the sanctuary.*

Ugly as Sin

Perhaps the most common elements of the nave are the pews (wooden benches with backs) and their kneelers. The traditional arrangement of the pews is unidirectional, that is, one behind the next, facing the sanctuary.[36] These marching rows of pews are what form that central aisle from narthex to sanctuary. They help define the road our pilgrim will take to approach the altar to receive the Holy Sacrament. They contribute to making a church *look like* a church as much as function like a church, rather than simply like a meeting hall.

Pews are a part of our Catholic patrimony and have commonly been used in the West since at least the thirteenth century, when they were designed as backless benches. By the late sixteenth century, because of the Counter Reformation's emphasis on preaching long sermons, most Catholic churches being built included wooden pews with kneelers and high backs. The new designs accommodated long periods of sitting. But even before full pews were commonly used, the faithful knelt during much of the Mass.

Kneeling, in fact, has always been a distinct posture for Catholic prayer:[37] in reverence and adoration of Christ, in supplication,

---

[36] In some large pilgrimage churches, pews are either movable or they're not used. In St. Peter's Basilica, for instance, chairs are used or else no seats are provided. This arrangement, however, is certainly not the norm in Catholic worship, but rather an exception precipitated by space necessities, since very large congregations often attend Masses and other ceremonies at St. Peter's.

[37] Kneeling is also a central posture of prayer in Scripture: "And a leper came to Him beseeching Him, and kneeling said to Him, 'If You will, You can make me clean'" (Mark 1:40). "And when Jesus came to the place He said to them, 'Pray that you may not enter into temptation.' And He withdrew from them about a stone's throw, and knelt down and prayed" (Luke 22:40-41). "And as they were stoning Stephen, he prayed, 'Lord Jesus, receive my spirit.' And he knelt down and cried with a loud voice, 'Lord, do not hold this sin against

and as a posture of humility. Through such a posture of the body, humbleness of heart is expressed, as are penitence and sorrow for sins committed. In fact, the early Church Fathers equated kneeling with prayer and worship. Eusebius, for instance, once wrote that St. James's continual kneeling in prayer gave him "knees as callous as those of a camel."[38] And Origen maintained that kneeling is necessary when forgiveness is sought.[39] With this in mind, our pilgrim, as a penitent, genuflects, kneeling briefly on one or both knees, before taking his place in a pew. The genuflection expresses a reverence and adoration of Christ in the Blessed Sacrament, either reserved in the tabernacle or exposed in a monstrance for adoration. This initial genuflection reflects an attitude of the heart, a prayerful and reverential one that prepares our pilgrim to offer adoration, thanksgiving, reparation, and supplication, through private devotion and prayers as well as to help celebrate the Holy Sacrifice of the Mass through the Liturgy.

Thus, Catholic worship — both in private devotion and in public liturgy — embraces both adoration and the humbling of ourselves before God. In the Liturgy, for instance, the Church calls for the faithful to kneel during the Eucharistic Prayer, when bread and wine are transubstantiated into the Body, Blood, soul, and divinity of Jesus Christ. The pew is meant to accommodate

them' " (Acts 7:59-60). "Peter put them all outside and knelt down and prayed; then turning to the body he said, 'Tabitha, rise' " (Acts 9:40). It's also a posture of prayer in the Old Testament: "[King Solomon] knelt upon his knees in the presence of all the assembly of Israel, and spread forth his hands toward heaven" (2 Chron. 6:13). "I rose from my fasting, with my garments and my mantle rent, and fell upon my knees and spread out my hands to the Lord my God" (Ezra 9:5). "[Daniel] got down on his knees three times a day and prayed and gave thanks before his God" (Dan. 6:10).

[38] From the May 1 reading in the old Roman Breviary.

[39] *De Orat*, 31.

and encourage this particular posture of worship. As such, it has become a memorable part of our churches.

⌒

The traditional church's confessional
prepares us to receive the Eucharist

Tied in with the posture of kneeling and with interior iconography is another important element of the nave: the confessional, where the penitent (that pilgrim who is repentant of his sins and seeks the forgiveness of God) solemnly receives the sacrament of Penance. The word *penance* is derived from the Latin word *poenitentia*, meaning sorrow, regret, and change of heart. Penance is also called the sacrament of conversion, the sacrament of Confession, the sacrament of forgiveness, and the sacrament of Reconciliation. This sacrament itself is a journey from conversion of heart to reconciliation with Christ and the Church. The confessional, then, appropriately makes provision for the posture of kneeling, which is logically the primary posture for sacramental Confession.

St. Charles Borromeo, writing in his seminal *Instructiones* on church architecture, developed the use of what we now consider the traditional wooden confessional "box," with a kneeler for the penitent and a screen placed between him and the priest confessor. St. Charles recommended that confessionals be placed at the sides of the nave in some clear, open space. He also recommended that the penitent be facing the sanctuary — if possible, turned toward the altar, the focal point of the church — when confessing and receiving the sacrament. After all, the sacrament of Penance is a preparation and strengthening on the pilgrimage road toward the sacrament of the Holy Eucharist, toward which all seven sacraments are ordered and that which is the source and summit of the Christian life. This pilgrimage is one directed toward maintaining a healthy spiritual life. Thus, the sacrament of Penance, given an architectural setting in an open part of the nave, serves to

St. Charles Borromeo developed the use of what we now consider the
wooden confessional "box," with a kneeler for the penitent and a screen
placed between him and the priest confessor. He recommended that
confessionals be placed at the sides of the nave in some clear, open space.

invite the pilgrim to prepare for the Holy Eucharist through conversion and repentance. "Penance," wrote Pope John Paul II, "leads to the Eucharist."[40]

Just as the baptismal font provided an iconographic object to represent the sacrament of Baptism, the confessional provides an opportunity to represent Penance. Following St. Charles Borromeo's recommendations, many Baroque churches, those built in the seventeenth and eighteenth centuries especially, have elaborate examples of woodwork with columns and carved images. The figures of Moses and Christ as well as the tablets of the Ten Commandments were often used in confessional imagery. Yet, no matter how plain a confessional might be, it should always reflect the dignity and solemnity of the sacrament. To this end, in place of figural imagery, columns are often used in the design.

The traditional church's columns
enhance its verticality and permanence

The column itself, in fact, plays a significant role in the arrangement and feel of the entire nave. First, its use in arcades on either side of the nave emphasizes the central aisle as a processional route, that road to Jerusalem. The regularly spaced columns help focus the sight lines on the sanctuary and the altar at the head of the building, at the "end of the road." They also help provide a sense of proper proportion, and for that reason, wrote Ralph Adams Cram, they shouldn't be dispensed with because of a "prejudice against seats behind columns," inherited from the Puritans. He added, "This prejudice against columns that cut off a direct view of the altar and pulpit from a few seats in the side aisles does not seem to be one which is based on reason. Not only does the omission of these arcades of columns and arches militate very

---

[40] *Dominicae cenae* (February 24, 1980), no. 7.

Columns have always provided buildings with a "sense of just proportion"
as well as a sense of dignity and solemnity, fitting for religious ritual.

seriously against the dignity and impressiveness of a church interior, it also is almost certain, particularly in the case of large churches, to destroy all sense of just proportion."[41]

Columns have always provided buildings, starting with Greek and Egyptian temples, with "a sense of just proportion" as well as a sense of dignity and solemnity — fitting for religious ritual. The Puritan meetinghouse prejudice addressed by Cram is against columns, piers, or any other architectural feature that would differentiate the structure from a lecture hall.

Columns have a long, rich history as used in the church building. We could devote several volumes to this topic alone, discussing the significance of the column's size, shape, shaft, head, and base, for example. But for our purposes here, suffice it to say that the column, when used properly in a colonnade or arcade, emphasizes the verticality of the nave, whether using the heavy stone columns of a Romanesque basilica or the tall, slender columns ("ribbons of rock strung between earth and sky"[42]) of a Gothic church. The column is an undeniably vertical element. As a structural element helping to support the weight of the building, it emphasizes the durability of the structure. And inasmuch as the column provides ample surface area, sculptors can mold these pillars into iconographic elements. The Apostles, for instance, who are called "pillars" of the church, especially Sts. Peter and Paul, appear in many churches as columns bearing the weight of the church.

The traditional church's pulpit is subordinate to the altar
Our pilgrim is uplifted by the beautiful pulpit from which the priest proclaims the Gospel and delivers his homily in clear hearing and in sight of all those present at the Mass. The pulpit is

[41] Cram, *Church Building*, 53.
[42] Temko, *Notre-Dame of Paris*, 144.

hexagonal and thus includes five reliefs (the sixth side is an opening to the lectern). The scenes depicted provide a continuous narrative with the Annunciation and the Nativity (together), the Adoration of the Magi, the Presentation in the Temple, the Crucifixion, and the Last Judgment. The pulpit is supported by a central column on a base with grotesque figures representing pagan elements subdued by Christianity. Six external columns are supported on the backs of lions that hover over vanquished prey, a motif symbolic of triumphant Christianity.

One function of the Liturgy now proper to both clergy and laity is proclaiming the Word of God. Consequently the architectural setting for reading or chanting the Scriptures — pulpit or ambo — is sometimes found in the nave, the realm of the laity, or at the entrance to the sanctuary, the realm of clerics and their attendants, i.e., "altar servers."

The placement of the pulpit in the nave, however, preceded the twentieth-century innovation of lay readers. Its placement reflected several considerations. The first was audibility. When a new church was built, at least from the twelfth century onward, a temporary pulpit would be constructed and used, so that it might be moved around until the best acoustical position had been found. Usually this was at the side of the nave nearer the sanctuary, either freestanding or built into a side wall or column. A horizontal piece was often placed above the head of the reader in order for his voice to project better to the congregation. This acoustical device, sometimes shaped like a shell or the sails of a ship, is called a *sounding board*. And, of course, the raised platform not only helps acoustically, but it also enables the congregation to see the priest or reader better.

Usually the Gospel pulpit was placed on the north side of the church (as was the baptistery), since the north symbolized paganism and darkness. It was large enough to accommodate the priest and his candle-bearers. On the south side, opposite the Gospel

*Pulpits lend themselves to ornamentation and properly become
another iconographic element of the church. They're crafted as works
of art, meant to inspire and to symbolize the preaching of the Word.*

pulpit, was often the Epistle pulpit. It was invariably smaller and less ornate than its Gospel counterpart.

A second consideration for placement of the pulpit was reverence and respect for Christ as symbolized by the altar and truly present in the tabernacle. Each pulpit was situated so that the preacher or reader would look out diagonally across the congregation. This enabled him never to have his back to the altar, the tabernacle, or — in cathedrals — to the bishop when present.

In the early Christian centuries, churches featured an ambo instead of a pulpit. The ambo was an elevated lectern, usually made of marble. It was reached by a flight of steps on either side. One flight was used to ascend and the other to descend. Only the Gospel was read from the ambo, since the bishop (and later priests also) usually preached from his chair. In the thirteenth century, however, the "preaching orders" of the Dominicans and the Franciscans placed a great emphasis on preaching sermons. It was then that the pulpit developed as a large and elaborate part of the church building, although never in competition with the altar (just as preaching wasn't considered in opposition to the eucharistic sacrifice). These larger pulpits lent themselves to ornamentation and properly became another iconographic element of the church. They were often crafted as works of art, meant to inspire and to symbolize the preaching of the Word. Some were domed, while others were covered with a small canopy or tester that functioned as a sounding board.

The traditional church's choir serves the Mass
without calling attention to itself

During the chanting of the *Credo* after the priest's homily, our pilgrim is again called into prayer and contemplation through his senses. This time, just as with the bells on his journey toward the church, he's called through his sense of sound. The voices of the choir ring out from above, resounding beautifully off the walls and ceiling of the church, which seem to be designed especially for sung chant and organ. Since he doesn't see the choir, our pilgrim, too, participates in the chant by singing while focusing his attention on the altar and the tabernacle in the sanctuary.

Choir is a name not only for a group of people but also for that place in the church set aside for those members of the congregation who are specially trained to lead the sung portion of the Liturgy. For acoustical reasons, choirs are typically placed on one of the building's axes. In many large ancient churches, especially the grand Gothic cathedrals such as Notre Dame, the choir is made up of a series of stalls at the front part of the nave, near the sanctuary. These were built at a time when the singers were made up exclusively of clerics, those of minor or major orders. (It wasn't until the Renaissance that choirs were laicized.)

The Council of Trent spent a long time considering the general state of sacred music.[43] One result of its deliberations affected the placement of the choir. Because of the council's recommendations, it gradually became the norm for the choir to be situated in the rear gallery, above the narthex or on a balcony that extends out over the rear of the nave. This distinct place of the nave has come to be known as the choir loft. The main purpose of the choir

---

[43] Prior to the Council of Trent, the general state of music in the Liturgy was seen as deteriorating. The sacred music, because it began to imitate popular forms of music, was robbed of all spiritual meaning. When the council convened in 1545 to consider various matters affecting the Church, the relationship of music to the Liturgy was among the many subjects discussed. In fact, much of the council's final year was devoted to studying sacred forms of music. As a result, Giovanni Pierluigi da Palestrina, who was known as the greatest composer of sacred music during the Renaissance, was commissioned to revise the Gregorian chants. His new versions provided the music that popes heard every day for centuries.

*For acoustical reasons, the choir is situated in
the rear gallery, above the narthex or on a balcony
that extends out over the rear of the nave.*

is to chant those portions of the Mass which vary with the week or
liturgical season and which can't usually be chanted by the entire
congregation. Yet congregational singing is strongly reinforced
when the organ and the well-trained voices of the choir lead from
above and behind. Thus, the choir and organ are placed in a rear
loft for acoustical reasons meant to enhance the quality of liturgical chant.

Since the voices of the choir are perceived audibly — our pilgrim *hears* them — it's neither necessary nor desired that the members of the choir be visible to the rest of the congregation. They're present at Holy Mass as worshipers, *not* entertainers. In other words, there's no serious reason why the rest of the congregation needs to see the choir throughout the course of the Liturgy. The rest of the congregation needs to hear the choir, and since the members of the choir, too, are worshipers, it's most appropriate that they face the same direction as the remainder of the worshiping congregation — toward the altar of sacrifice. Furthermore, the "disembodied voices" of the choir are often perceived as heavenly voices from above, the chant of a choir of angels.

⤳

The traditional church's sacred art teaches and evangelizes us

In the twelfth century, Abbot Suger of St. Denis wrote that "art leads minds from material to immaterial things." Our pilgrim in the nave of the church isn't unaffected by the environment of sacred art. Statuary, stained-glass windows, side-aisle shrines, and other devotional art in the form of reliefs, mosaics, frescoes, or murals are all designed to raise our minds and spirits to God and to things eternal. It's sacred art that helps the architecture of our churches to awe and inspire. Such art prepares our pilgrim to humble himself before God, to offer his prayers and adoration, to prepare to celebrate Holy Mass, and to approach the altar to receive the Holy Sacrament. It enhances the architecture and the Liturgy, and it lifts our pilgrim's mind to God through its beauty and meaning.

As mentioned previously, the iconography of sacred art, just like the iconography of the architecture itself, teaches and evangelizes. In fact, sacred art is placed at the service of the Church: it's an intimate component of Catholic worship, both public (in the Liturgy) and private (in devotion).

Sacred art helps church architecture to awe and inspire. It prepares the pilgrim to humble himself before God, to offer prayers and adoration, to prepare to celebrate Mass, and to approach the altar to receive the Holy Sacrament.

In 1963, Pope Paul VI recognized this fact formally at the Second Vatican Council. The fine arts, the council fathers wrote, and the Pope ratified, "are considered to rank among the noblest expressions of human genius." *Sacred* art, they continued, is the highest achievement in art, because it's related to God's boundless beauty: "To the extent that these works aim exclusively at turning men's thoughts to God persuasively and devoutly, they are dedicated to God and to the cause of His greater honor and glory."[44]

[44] *Sacrosanctum Concilium*, no. 122.

Throughout the Christian centuries, the Popes have always reiterated this point, especially when the Byzantine Iconoclasts of the eighth and ninth centuries violently challenged the use of figural imagery in sacred art. St. John Damascene provided the strongest argument against the destruction of images, claiming that ultimately the Iconoclasts denied the fundamental doctrine of the Incarnation, that God was made flesh. Christ Himself, by His human birth, made it possible to represent Him in sacred art. For this reason, among others, the Second Council of Nicea declared that Iconoclasm, the belief that figural imagery encouraged idolatrous worship and should therefore be forbidden, was a heresy.

The figural image, in fact, is a primary vessel of meaning in the house of God. Drawing on the great treasury of symbolic heroes from the Bible — prophets and patriarchs — and Church history, with its saints who provide models of virtue in every vocation and walk of life in imitation of Christ, sacred art conveys meaning on several levels.

First, the figure or image conveys a *historical* meaning. For instance, in the portrayal of Abraham lifting his knife to slay his only son, Isaac, only to be held back by an angelic messenger from God, our pilgrim can reflect on the historical account in Scripture: God instructed Abraham to sacrifice his only son; Abraham rose early the next morning, and, taking Isaac with him on his saddled ass, he climbed Mount Moriah and prepared wood for the burnt offering. Just when Abraham was about to slay his son, an angel of the Lord appeared to stay his hand, and a ram replaced Isaac as the sacrificial offering.[45]

The second meaning is *symbolic*. Often Old Testament scenes symbolize New Testament events. The sacrifice of Isaac, the only son of Abraham, prefigures the Sacrifice of Christ, the only Son of

---

[45] Cf. Gen. 22.

Sacred art is placed at the service of the Church; it's an intimate component of Catholic worship, both public (in the Liturgy) and private (in devotion).

God. From eternity God wanted His only Son to shed His Blood for the salvation of man.

The third meaning is *allegorical*. The figural images are used to represent moral principles, themes, or virtues. Abraham's sacrifice of Isaac represents, for example, self-denial, fear of the Lord, and obedience to the will of God. Literature, most obviously in the Scriptures, carries these same layers of meaning. In sacred Christian art, as with Scripture, these meanings are always Christological; in other words, they're always centered on Christ.

Beyond these layers of meaning, there's beauty as well, but no true sacred art can be simply beautiful, detached from the meaning it carries. In a church, the purpose of beauty is to make the truths represented attractive to the senses. And if these beautifully represented truths are Christological, they'll aid our pilgrim in prayer, meditation, contemplation, and in the ultimate form of Christian worship: participating in the Holy Sacrifice of the Mass.

The richness of sacred art, however, isn't limited to the figural image, although that is its most popular form throughout the majority of Christian epochs. Meaning in sacred art is also expressed by the use of specific objects or nonhuman figures, such as fruit, books, skulls, and candles. The language of signs and symbols, according to art historian George Ferguson, is "the outward and visible form through which is revealed the inward and invisible reality that moves and directs the soul of a man."[46] The greatest and most common of Christian symbols is, of course, the Cross, which universally represents the whole of the Christian Faith. It also points to Christ's sacrifice and God's love for man in the sacrifice of His Son for the salvation of the world.

Early Christians, through fear of persecution, were forced to develop more circumspect symbols than the Cross. They used

---

[46] George Ferguson, *Signs and Symbols in Christian Art* (New York: Oxford University Press, 1954), xi.

common objects and animals such as the fish and the anchor to represent Christ. The same was true for representing other spiritual truths. The dove, for instance, was used then, as it is today, to represent the Holy Spirit — clearly a Scriptural allusion: "The heavens were opened and He saw the Spirit of God descending like a dove."[47]

Throughout the following centuries, Christian artists developed a rich system of Catholic symbols. By the Renaissance, these signs and symbols were ordered so that their meanings might be universally understood. The lily, for instance, represents purity and is a symbol of the Immaculate Conception. The camel, because it could go without drink for long periods of time, symbolizes temperance. The ox, an animal commonly used by the Jews for holocausts, stands for sacrifice, and the ass, which sometimes accompanies the ox in Nativity images, stands for humility.

Not only are truths, virtues, and Christian principles represented by symbols, but saints are also identified by the objects they bear when portrayed in sacred art. St. Peter is recognized by his keys, which represent the papacy in Scripture through the *traditio clavium*: "You are Peter, and on this rock I will build my church. . . . I will give you the keys of the kingdom of Heaven."[48]

*The traditional church's stained glass
creates a heavenly atmosphere with light*

Another common and important form of sacred imagery is the tall stained-glass windows that line the side walls of the nave. The Benedictine Abbot Suger called them "radiant windows to illumine men's minds so that they may travel through the light to an apprehension of God's light." He also called them "sermons that

---

[47] Matt. 3:16.
[48] Matt. 16:18-19.

Abbot Suger called stained-glass windows the "most radiant
windows to illumine men's minds so that they may
travel through the light to an apprehension of God's light."

reached the heart through the eyes instead of entering through the ears." Thus did the abbot describe the use of stained glass for sacred purposes. Inspired by this abbot, Gothic architects popularized this artistic method and used this mysterious light to obtain a feeling of aspiration toward God and Heaven. Such has come to be the norm throughout centuries since.

Stained-glass windows are composed of small pieces of colored glass held together in strips of cast lead to form images that tell the story of salvation history. Stained glass is unique in that it's the only art form that relies entirely on natural daylight. Every other art form, such as painting and sculpture, is designed to be seen by reflected light. With a stained-glass window, however, the artist designs it so that the artistic effect is created by light passing through the glass. In a manner of speaking, the artist must "paint" with the light of God. When the sun shines through these windows, the light is transformed into multicolored patterns on the interior of the church, creating an other-worldly feel, a hint at the beauty of Heaven.

A great many Christian images and symbols — probably as many as exist — have been depicted in stained glass. The imagery of the saints, of Christ, and of the Blessed Virgin have been used and developed in the stained-glass images. The Bible and the lives of the saints were the two main inspirations for the donors who commissioned glaziers to create these "poems in glass."

The sanctuary sets apart the holiest part of the church

Just as all the sacraments are ordered toward the Holy Eucharist, the ark of salvation is ordered toward the *sanctuary*. Every aspect of the nave — pews, furnishings, architectural elements, and sacred art — ultimately leads to the sanctuary, the place in the church built especially for the altar of sacrifice. This is the Christian equivalent to the "Holy of Holies" of the tabernacle in the wilderness and in Solomon's Temple.[49] Although the sanctuary represents the apex of our pilgrim's journey and the summit of the Liturgy, the pilgrim merely approaches it. It isn't his dwelling place; it is God's.

In the Temple of Jerusalem, the sanctuary was also God's dwelling place, and only the ordained entered this most sacred of places: "While [Zechariah] was serving as priest before God when his division was on duty, according to the custom of the priesthood, it fell to him by lot to enter the temple of the Lord and burn incense. And the multitude of the people were praying outside at the hour of incense."[50] In like manner, the Christian sanctuary has always been the place for the clergy and those assisting the clergy at Mass, just as the nave is the place for the non-ordained faithful, whether praying the Rosary, adoring the Blessed Sacrament, or participating in the Liturgy of the Mass.

In this way, our pilgrim is reminded that the Church is hierarchical, composed of different members — the head being Christ; with Pope, bishops, and priests each serving as *alter Christus*, "another Christ"; and with the religious and laity serving their own functions as part of the Church Militant.[51] That hierarchy is reflected in the Liturgy on earth as it is in Heaven. In an *ad limina* address in 1998, Pope John Paul II reminded a group of U.S. bishops that "the Liturgy, like the Church, is intended to be hierarchical and polyphonic, respecting the different roles assigned by Christ and allowing all the different voices to blend together into one great hymn of praise."[52] It only follows, then, that if the Church

---

[49] Cf. Heb. 9:3 ff.

[50] Luke 1:8-9.

[51] That is, the members of the Church on earth. The members in Heaven are known as the Church Triumphant and the members in Purgatory as the Church Suffering.

[52] *Ad limina* address to the Bishops of Washington, Oregon, and Alaska, October 9, 1998.

*Every aspect of the nave — pews, furnishings, architectural
elements, and sacred art — ultimately leads to the sanctuary,
the place in the church built especially for the altar of sacrifice.*

and the Liturgy are both hierarchical, the church building ought to reflect that hierarchy. This logic is reflected by the Church's stipulation that the "sanctuary should be marked off from the nave by a higher floor level and by a distinctive structure or decor."[53]

To put it simply and to reiterate the point: the sanctuary is meant to be a *separate* place in the church. It's the place where the priest offers the Holy Sacrifice of the Mass and where the Blessed Sacrament is reserved for adoration, an extension of the Holy Sacrifice.

The sanctuary is a raised area primarily for two reasons. The first is figurative: since the sanctuary represents Christ the head (and also the head of Christ), it's only natural that the head be higher than the body. Second, the sanctuary is elevated for a practical reason: so that the congregation can easily see the different parts of the Liturgy that take place in the sanctuary. If the nave is ordered toward the sanctuary, our pilgrim ought to be able to see it from the nave.

The sanctuary is also marked off from the nave by a "distinctive structure." In many churches, the sanctuary is not only *differentiated* from the nave, but it's also framed by the triumphal arch, the portion of the wall over the arch that separates nave from sanctuary. The name is taken from the grand arches built by emperors or governments typically to commemorate a military conquest. Two of the most well-known arches are the nineteenth-century Arc de Triomphe in Paris and the fourth-century Arch of Constantine in Rome. The first is a single grand arch, whereas the second is formed by a large central arch flanked by two smaller ones. Both forms have been adapted to churches. The triple-opening arch was applied to those churches that have small side apses or chapels flanking the central apse of the sanctuary. The single-opening arch was used even since the first basilicas built in Rome. The oldest is probably the triumphal arch of Santa Maria Maggiore (435),

---

[53] *General Instruction of the Roman Missal*, no. 258.

The sanctuary is marked off from the nave by a "distinctive structure" commonly called the communion rail. It not only serves to define the sanctuary, but it is functional as well. Here the pilgrim, approaching the altar, kneels to receive the Holy Eucharist in adoration and humility.

which is decorated by mosaics that portray narrative scenes from the life of Christ.

Another common structure is the *communion rail*, or *altar rail*, usually a low balustrade made of carved wood, stone, wrought iron, stainless steel, or other precious materials. It not only serves to define the sanctuary; it is functional as well. Here our pilgrim, approaching the altar, kneels to receive the Holy Eucharist in adoration and humility.[54] At times outside of Mass, the pilgrim can

[54] Although in some places the practice of kneeling at the altar rail to receive Communion has fallen by the wayside, it's still

give thanksgiving here, praying before the Blessed Sacrament in the tabernacle or exposed on the altar. At the rail, as in the pews, our pilgrim has the opportunity to assume the traditional Catholic posture of worship: kneeling.

From the sixteenth century to the late twentieth century, communion rails were almost universal in Catholic churches where the Roman rite is followed. Before the sixteenth century, in place of the communion rail, there was a low wall that functioned in much the same way as the balustrade and effectively separated the sanctuary from the nave without the two areas appearing or being disconnected. Even in fourth-century basilicas, these low walls, called *cancelli*, were extant. Since the faithful began to kneel at the rail for Communion, the altar rail has been understood as an extension of the altar, where the Holy Sacrifice of the Mass takes place, just as the reserved Blessed Sacrament is an extension of the Mass. For this reason, the design of the railing reflects the design and construction of the altar.

Finally, because the infinite act of the ultimate sacrifice is offered here, the sanctuary is differentiated by its decor. Sacred art and architectural elements, including the sanctuary's furnishings, express the majesty, grandeur, and sublimity of the Sacred Mystery enacted. St. Charles Borromeo, who called the sanctuary the "Chapel of the High Altar," recommended that the ceiling of the sanctuary be vaulted or at least be built of a rarer and richer form and material than that of the nave. The walls should be richly decorated with mosaics, paintings, frescoes, or stained glass. And all should "be proportioned to express harmonious unity."

a normative method of reception. In *Eucharisticum Mysterium* (Instruction on the Worship of the Eucharistic Mystery, 1967) Pope Paul VI wrote, "When the faithful communicate kneeling, no other sign of reverence toward the Blessed Sacrament is required, since kneeling is itself a sign of adoration" (no. 34).

*In many churches, the sanctuary is not only differentiated from
the nave, but is framed by the triumphal arch, the portion of the wall
over the arch or arches that separates the nave from the sanctuary.*

*The traditional church's altar is the focal point
of unity, reverence, prayer, and worship*

In a manner of speaking, the entire church ought to reflect the
design of the altar, since the church building is actually built *for the
altar* rather than the altar being just another furnishing in the
house of God. The altar is the focal point of unity, reverence,
prayer, and worship. To it all things are tributary, and at the same
time, it's the soul of the entire organism. This is the reason why all

sight lines in the building naturally lead to the altar, why all pews face in one direction toward the altar, why the kneeling penitent faces the altar in the confessional, and why the Liturgy reaches its climax at the Consecration, when, through the hands of the anointed priest, the bread and wine are transubstantiated into the Body, Blood, soul, and divinity of Jesus Christ.

Architect Ralph Adams Cram explained it this way: "Every line, every mass, every detail, is so conceived and disposed that it exalts the altar, that it leads to it, as any work of art leads to its just climax. By the lines of arcades, the curves of arch and vault, the ranged windows, and the gathering chapels and aisles with their varied lights and shadows, the eye, and through the eye the mind, and through the mind the soul, is led onward step by step until it rests on the altar itself."[55]

The sacrificial altar is so important and central to Catholic worship, not primarily because it's a table on which a banquet is prepared, but because this is where the priest re-presents Christ's Sacrifice on the Cross. The altar, in fact, not only represents the Last Supper and the Sacrifice of the Cross, but Christ Himself, who is the Victim of this ultimate Sacrifice. The Church recognizes this by defining the altar as "a sign of Christ Himself, the place at which the saving mysteries are carried out, and the center of the assembly, to which the greatest reverence is due."[56]

The Latin word *altare*, from which is derived *altar*, literally means "a place of sacrifice." The word *sacrifice*, in turn, is derived from the Latin, meaning "to make holy." The principal purpose of sacrifice is to give honor and glory to God. It's the highest form of worship, which was central to almost all religions throughout history and is certainly central to Catholicism through the Holy Sacrifice of the Mass, the most perfect of all sacrifices.

[55] Cram, *Church Building*, 151.
[56] Pope Paul VI, *Eucharisticum Mysterium*, no. 24.

*The altar is the focal point of unity, reverence, prayer,
and worship. To it all things are tributary, and at
the same time, it's the soul of the entire organism.*

Accordingly, in the vast majority of churches built in the past two thousand years, the altar is centered in the sanctuary, either freestanding or built up against a wall with a decorative structure, e.g., a reredos, retablo, or altarpiece, behind. When Christians gained freedom of public worship in the fourth century, permanent altars, usually made of stone, were erected for the first time in Europe. In those days, the veneration of the martyrs, who had died for Christ, was so great that almost every church in those years, especially in Rome, was built over the tomb of a martyr; and the church took the name of that saint — for instance, St. Peter's Basilica. Because of this tradition, relics of the saints were placed within a part of the altar called the sepulchrum; and until recently altars were required to hold the authenticated relics of at least two canonized saints.

The most important aspect of the altar, however, is the plain horizontal stone slab on which the priest places the Holy Sacrifice. At its consecration by a bishop, this stone, which is a symbol of Christ, is marked with five crosses, symbolic of Christ's wounds: one cross in each corner and another on the cover of the reliquary sepulchrum. The use of stone not only recalls the stone altars commissioned by God Himself in the Old Testament as well as those used in the Roman catacombs before the Edict of Milan, but it's also a symbol of Christ, "the Stone which the builders rejected."[57] Accordingly, St. John Chrysostom once wrote, "This altar is an object of wonder: by nature it is stone."[58]

Although the earliest stone altars were simple slabs supported by columns, blocks, or sarcophagi, in later centuries the supporting stonework was often carved with reliefs of the Last Supper, the Sacrifice of Abraham, or other sacrificial imagery. Thus, the altar not only maintains pride of place in the church, but its

---

[57] Ps. 118:22-23; Matt. 21:42.
[58] Quoted in the Church's *Dedication of a Church and an Altar*.

ornamentation also speaks volumes of its primary importance. The altar, like the baptismal font, the confessional, and the pews, became an iconographic object, using figural images and Christian symbolism.

Since the altar is relatively small in comparison with the size of its church, it's surrounded with pleasing accessories that draw the eye, the mind, and the soul to this piece of stone. For instance, it's often adorned with altar linens of intricate needlework, with candlesticks, and with a crucifix. In the most fortunate churches, a grand wooden, stone, or metal canopy is built over the altar. This is called a *baldacchino*. It consists usually of four columns supporting a dome-like top that sits over the altar. Arguably, there's no better way to draw attention to a freestanding altar. Often resembling a jeweled crown, it's a symbol of the authority and kingship of Christ. Similar canopies made of textile and supported on poles were once held over Byzantine emperors during processions as a sign of their dignity and authority.[59] Likewise, in pagan basilicas, a similar canopy surmounted the chief magistrate's seat as a symbol of his authority derived from the Roman emperor. As such, the baldacchino emphasizes the dignity and majesty of the altar as representing Christ Himself.

These beautiful structures have been used since the fourth century, when Constantine had one erected over the high altar of the Basilica of St. John Lateran. Today, all of the Roman basilicas have ornate baldacchinos, the most acclaimed being that of St. Peter's, designed by Bernini, a masterful feat of engineering, architecture, and monumental sculpture.

In other churches where a freestanding altar isn't used or where a baldacchino can't be used, a decorative structure built behind

---

[59] A portable baldacchino made out of textile is carried over the exposed Blessed Sacrament during eucharistic processions, such as during Forty Hours celebrations and on Corpus Christi.

the altar serves the same purposes of decoration and demarcation. These structures take two main forms: the reredos and the altarpiece. The reredos is a great screen of statuary niches and sculptured panels that rises from the back of the altar. It commonly contains architectural, sculptural, and painted components. Gothic reredoses were also commonly designed with fretted pinnacles, resembling those exterior elements adjunct to the flying buttress and resembling spires. These medieval reredoses often resembled the Gothic façades. In the Baroque era, the reredos became quite elaborate, especially in Spain and Latin America, where it's known by the Spanish term *retablo*. Extensively decorated with carved polychrome figures, the Latin American retablos combined the solomonic column form from St. Peter's Basilica with stone sculpture, painted tiles, stuccowork, and frescoes.

By comparison, the altarpiece is made up of fewer images and figures but is ideally equal in beauty. It consists of paintings, carved panels, or both, usually reflecting the dedication of the church to a particular saint. Some are more elaborate, showing various narrative scenes from the life of Christ or the life of Mary. Siena Cathedral, dedicated to the Virgin, for instance, has a painted altarpiece known as the *Maesta*. The main scene is that of Madonna and Child surrounded by angels and saints, while smaller paintings depict scenes from the life of Christ.

Sculptural altarpieces such as Bernini's *Ecstasy of St. Teresa* in Santa Maria della Vittoria, are a product of the Counter Reformation Baroque. Other altarpieces are made up of separate panels that are hinged together: a diptych contains two, a triptych three, and a polyptych four or more. One of the most acclaimed polyptychs is the altarpiece known as *Adoration of the Lamb* at St. Bevon Church in Ghent, Belgium, painted by Flemish brothers Hubert and Jan Van Eyck.

The majority of post-Reformation churches include the tabernacle as an integral, if not central, part of the reredos or altarpiece,

In the most fortunate churches, a grand wooden, stone, or metal
canopy is built over the altar. This is called a baldacchino. It consists
usually of four columns supporting a dome-like top that sits over the altar.
Arguably there's no better way to draw attention to a freestanding altar.

*The reredos is a great screen of statuary niches and sculpted panels
that rises from the back of the altar. It commonly contains
architectural, sculptural, and painted components.*

giving it due prominence and an essential intimacy with the altar of sacrifice.

☞

The crucifix tells us of Christ's redemptive Sacrifice

Another integral feature of the sanctuary is the crucifix, which Abbot Suger called "the health-bringing banner of the eternal victory of our Savior."[60] The most common of all Christian subjects depicted in art is the crucifixion, which is described by all four evangelists.[61] Since the Mass is integrally bound up in the Sacrifice of Christ on the Cross, a crucifix is inseparable from the Liturgy, from the altar, and from the church. Quite simply, a crucifix is an object of meditation, contemplation, and veneration in the shape of a cross, with a corpus of Christ that shows His five wounds — in both hands, in both feet, and in His side. This simple artistic and liturgical object recalls Jesus' death, Resurrection, and Ascension into glory; it expresses the total and universal Paschal Mystery of Christ; and it invites the pilgrim to take part in it with a lively and lived faith.

Our pilgrim meditates on the Incarnation, the Lord's act of wholly assuming the form of a man; he contemplates the suffering Christ endured on the Cross through His wounds and suffocation; he venerates the Cross as a symbol of Christ's redemption of man through this Sacrifice to end all sacrifices. The position of the crucifix hanging above and behind the altar reminds our pilgrim that this redemptive sacrifice is what is being re-presented through the Holy Sacrifice of the Mass by the hands of the ordained priest.

Since the crucifix is the symbol par excellence for the Christian, its appearance is of great importance in the church. It's large

[60] Abbot Suger, *The Book of Suger, Abbot of Saint-Denis,* "Of the Golden Crucifix," sect. XXXII, paragraph 1.
[61] Matt. 27; Mark 15; Luke 23; John 19.

enough not only to be seen by the faithful but to be contemplated as well, particularly during the Eucharistic Prayer. Since at least the thirteenth century in the West, Christ has been depicted as visibly suffering, His wounds visible.[62] Such graphic depictions help our pilgrim to understand that crucifixion was one of the cruelest, most humiliating forms of punishment in the ancient world. The Jewish historian Josephus best described it following the siege of Jerusalem by the Romans in the years 66 to 70 as "the most wretched of deaths." In this way, the crucifix is an icon to be contemplated. In fact, it's the central icon of the Faith, an icon that invites our pilgrim to participate in the Cross of Christ. As the apostle Paul says, "Far be it from me to glory, except in the Cross of our Lord Jesus Christ."[63]

The tabernacle reminds us that Christ is truly present here

The *alpha* and the *omega* — the beginning and the end — of all things is Christ. This is, of course, particularly true of the church, the house of God. The mandate to make Christ present and active in any one place begins in a substantially real way with the Holy Sacrifice of the Mass, in which Jesus is made present — Body, Blood, soul, and divinity — on the sacred altar. Communion of the Holy Eucharist is food for our souls, but the Blessed Sacrament remains in the church even after the last Mass of the day. Thus, the Mass is extended by both reservation and exposition of the Host (the Holy Sacrifice). Consequently the tabernacle, which reserves the Blessed Sacrament all day, every day, is a necessary adjunct to the altar. Jesus is always present; He is always available in

---

[62] Pope Pius XII wrote, "One would be straying from the straight path . . . were he to order the crucifix so designed that the divine Redeemer's body shows no trace of His cruel sufferings": *Mediator Dei* (1947), nos. 61-64.

[63] Gal. 6:14.

Since the Mass is integrally bound up in the Sacrifice of Christ on the Cross, a crucifix is inseparable from the Liturgy, from the altar, and from the church.

this particularly real way. The reserved Blessed Sacrament renders the tabernacle the beating heart of the house of God, made possible by the altar and the ordained priest, both of which represent Christ, but are *not* Christ in Body, Blood, soul, and divinity.

The presence of Christ in the tabernacle is truly what separates the Catholic church building from all other buildings that have ever been built since the beginning of time. It's a call to prayer and an opportunity for our pilgrim to meet God in a unique way. Eucharistic adoration — kneeling and praying before the Blessed Sacrament — offers our pilgrim a way to be spiritually refreshed. The divine presence in the tabernacle satisfies his longing to be near Christ in a real way. This is why, throughout the day, pilgrims from far and near will come to the church to "pay a visit," kneeling for a time in silent prayer focusing on the eucharistic Christ. This "beating heart" is what truly gives life to the church. Consequently, the architectural setting for the reservation of Christ in the Blessed Sacrament is of highest importance. Thus, the tabernacle is prominently placed in relation to the altar, directly behind, for instance, often a part of the altarpiece or reredos. When our pilgrim first sets foot in the nave, perhaps even before he reaches out to bless himself with holy water, his eye instinctively gravitates toward the tabernacle and altar — inseparable — and immediately understands that he's truly in the presence of God on earth. Above or beside the tabernacle he sees the vigil lamp perpetually glowing in honor of Christ's presence and recognizes the veil as a sign that Christ in the Blessed Sacrament is indeed within.

The tabernacle veil, called a *canopeum*, hearkens back to the veil of the Holy of Holies, where the presence of God abided in the Old Covenant. The veil is split down the middle, recalling the veil of the Temple that was "torn in two, from top to bottom" at the hour of Christ's death.[64] In fact, the name *tabernacle* derives

---

[64] Cf. Matt. 27:51.

from *tabernaculum*, meaning "little tent of the Lord," the movable structure used to house the Ark of the Covenant.

Through eucharistic adoration and prayers of thanksgiving, our pilgrim prepares to "gird his loins," to take leave of the house of God and dwell again in the world, carrying both Christ's Cross and His grace out into his lived vocation. His life as a Christian flows from the font of the Mass and is fueled by the relationship of intimacy provided not only by the Blessed Sacrament reserved in the tabernacle or exposed on the altar, but also through the maternal sanctuary of the entire house of God whose architectural and artistic elements work together to perpetually call our pilgrim to return again and again.

The presence of Christ in the tabernacle is truly what separates
the Catholic church building from all other buildings
that have ever been built since the beginning of time.

Chapter Three

☞

Our pilgrim goes into the
worship space of the people
(or, why you find it so hard to pray
in that modern church)

As our pilgrim makes his way to the modern church, he must carry a detailed road map with him. He can't locate the modern church by means of a steeple or by following the sound of pealing bells. Accordingly, he neither sees an inviting spire nor hears a welcoming peal. Instead, he keeps alert for road signs to direct him to the modern church, which is inconspicuous, like a lamp hidden under a bushel.[65]

The modern church itself can't be seen from the boulevard, but a small sign near the road informs our pilgrim that a Catholic church lies beyond, off a wooded side street, but only after he has driven well past the drive. A break in the boulevard half a mile ahead allows the pilgrim to make a U-turn, and he drives back toward the church and beyond it to the next break in the boulevard, where he makes another U-turn and heads back toward the church, praying that he'll see the driveway entrance this time before he passes it.

[65] Cf. Matt. 5:14.

Ugly as Sin

Our pilgrim turns off the main boulevard onto the wooded side street that could be mistaken for a private driveway. Once past the parking lot of a nearby shopping plaza, he beholds in the distance among the pines a building resembling a conference center or maybe a school. It's hard to tell, but the addresses of the buildings nearby indicate that the modern church must be near. Soon a sign reading "Church Parking" instructs the pilgrim that this structure, built most obviously in the 1970s (probably in 1978, when the origami-style church was in fashion) is some kind of "house of worship." The road map confirms that this is the local modern Catholic church.

Our pilgrim notices that the modern church is rarely conspicuous, not by its form (there are no spires, domes, or cross-tipped bell towers), not by its location, and not by its beauty. Some, however, are conspicuous by virtue of their sheer ugliness or strangeness. In Oakland, for instance, the new cathedral is conspicuous inasmuch as it's the only building within miles that resembles a giant clamshell. The Cathedral in Rio de Janiero, a hulking concrete mass uniquely resembling a Mayan ziggurat or Death Star spacecraft right off the set of *Star Wars*, does little to remind our pilgrim of a house of God or a gate of Heaven, but he can't help but miss this most outrageous form rising from the flat landscape. Nor can he miss the huge tepee-like structure that is Brazil's Maringa Cathedral, or the water-cooling tower that is Brasilia's cathedral.

⁀

The modern church's façade doesn't
evangelize, teach, or catechize

Our pilgrim circles the parking lot, looking for an empty spot to park his car. Because he arrived late and the Mass began ten minutes before, he has some difficulty finding a spot. He walks quickly to the nearest entrance, up the zig-zagging handicap access ramp that leads to a rear door nearest his car. The parking lot

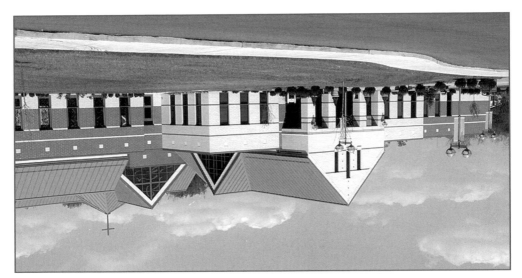

The façade, that is, the "face" the modern church presents to the world is "faceless." It doesn't evangelize, teach, or catechize.

Our pilgrim goes into the worship space and the entrance are no different from the outside world. Our pilgrim, instead of being disposed by the architecture to prepare himself for entrance into the house of God, remains distracted by the frustration of finding the modern church.

Let us, however, assume that our pilgrim goes to the main entrance to the modern church. Doing so, the building recedes into the background of the landscape. There's nothing memorable here. Nothing inspiring. Nothing particularly inviting. There's perhaps one unidentifiable statue, such as the short-haired Virgin Mary of the Los Angeles Cathedral, if there's any iconography at all. The landscaping, if done well with beautiful indigenous flowers, is probably the most memorable feature.

Our pilgrim finds that the façade, the "face" this church pre-sents to the world, is "faceless." It doesn't evangelize, teach, or

Ugly as Sin

catechize. It simply fits in more or less with the other buildings on that street. No passersby would be curious enough to go out of their way to explore this edifice; neither skeptic nor pious pilgrim will be drawn to its portals, attracted to or even intrigued by any inherent meaning. The faceless façade of the modern church fails to communicate meaning to anyone, because the exterior of the building is conceived of merely as a "skin for a liturgical action."[66] Its agnostic aesthetic embraces no particular doctrine, and its form is reflective neither of Catholic Tradition nor architectural history.

Designers and architects of the modern church are careful not to offend anyone in the community by using particularly Catholic symbols such as the crucifix or even the Latin cross. Following the modern church fashion of the 1990s, a circular window, barely reminiscent of a Romanesque oculus or a Gothic rose window, is divided into four panes to form a "Greek cross." Since the horizontal and vertical pieces of a Greek cross are equal in length, the Christian symbolism is lost in the window, and therefore it's doubtful that the frequent passerby will be offended by such inconspicuous Christian symbolism. Neither will the pilgrim immediately (or perhaps ever) perceive the Greek cross form. To everyone except the liturgist, the round window is nothing more than a round window with four panes of equal size.

An important element of the modern façade is the door (or doors) to the modern church. Concurrent with nearly all modern church design fashions is the concept of "welcoming doors." These take the form of transparent glass doors that resemble those

[66] "The norm for designing liturgical space is the assembly and its liturgies. The building or cover enclosing the architectural space is a shelter or 'skin' for a liturgical action. It does not have to 'look like' anything else, past or present": *Environment and Art in Catholic Worship* (Bishops' Committee on the Liturgy, 1978).

you'd find in other public buildings and in cheap restaurants. Sr. Sandra Schweitzer, who served as design consultant for architect Edward Sövik on the renovation of SS. Peter and Paul Cathedral in Indianapolis (1983-1986), explained, "With that project, we replaced the heavy, thick metal doors with interior glass doors that say, 'You're always welcome in here.' "[67] Accordingly, most

Following the modern church fashion of the 1990s,
a circular window is divided into four panes to form a
"Greek cross." Since the horizontal and vertical pieces
of a Greek cross are equal in length, the Christian
symbolism is lost in the window.

[67] Michael S. Rose, "Can Modern Churches Be Beautiful?" *National Catholic Register* (June 13-19, 1999).

Concurrent with nearly all modern church design fashions is the
concept of "welcoming doors." These take the form of transparent
glass doors that resemble those you'd find in other public buildings.

renovated churches lost their often ornate, if heavy, doors because church renovators deemed them "unwelcoming." How glass doors are more welcoming than opaque doors has never really been explained, but the use of these transparent portals conveys a sense of ordinariness and cheapness; it contributes to the feel that the building is not ecclesiastical, but secular; it fails to convey a sense of permanence or durability.

⌒

The modern church's gathering space
doesn't draw us toward the sanctuary

The modern church is unwilling to entertain the dark vestibules of older churches, but does provide a kind of secularized atrium, a transition room between the parking lot and the worship space. As our pilgrim enters through the welcoming doors, he finds himself in a vast empty space, except for the Jacuzzi-style baptismal font that may be the focal point of the room, depending on the fashion era of the church. This area, he quickly discovers, is a place for parishioners to gather before and after Mass. It's brightly lit and often quite barren. People are considered the furnishings here. Effectively the gathering space is a lobby. If devotional items are to be found here, they're inconspicuous, perhaps tucked away around the corner in a hallway that leads to the drinking fountain, the bathrooms, and a pay phone.

Sometimes our pilgrim finds that there are many hallways and closed doors that lead he knows not where. Sometimes offices are connected to the gathering space. Sometimes there are various chapels off the gathering space: the Blessed Sacrament chapel, the Reconciliation chapel, the day chapel, the marriage chapel, the funeral chapel, and so forth. Instead of bearing some significant relationship to the altar of the "worship space," these chapels are disconnected from the altar. If he arrives for a daily Mass, our pilgrim may enter the main worship space, with its barren wood altar,

The "gathering space" is a place for parishioners to gather
before and after Mass. It's brightly lit and often quite barren.
People are considered the furnishings here.

only to discover that he's in the wrong "room" of this sprawling complex. He's assured, however, by literature available just inside the glass doors that the layout of this modern church is "welcoming" and fulfills a mandate for "hospitality."[68]

In some renovated churches, our pilgrim finds that the former baptistery has been converted into a "devotional chapel." In this

---

[68] "[L]iturgy flourishes in a climate of hospitality: a situation in which people are comfortable with one another, either knowing or being introduced to one another; a space in which people are seated together, with mobility, in view of one another as well as the focal points of the rite": *Environment and Art in Catholic Worship*, no. 11.

room, he finds a gathering of the statues that once adorned the nave and the sanctuary of the church in its pre-renovation days. In St. Lawrence Church in Cincinnati, for instance, the saints all gather in the former baptistery as if convening to discuss the reason for their removal from the main body of the church.

⌒

The modern church's baptismal font suggests
hot-tub parties, not entrance into the Church

Depending on the year in which the modern church was designed or renovated, our pilgrim might find the baptismal font at the entrance to the modern church worship space, either in the center of the gathering space or at the back of the nave. In other words, the placement of the baptistery depends on the liturgical theory of the day. Renovators of the 1990s seemed willing to admit, for example, that their recommendations in the 1970s to locate the font in the sanctuary next to the altar, wasn't the best solution.

Liturgical design consultant Christine Reinhard writes in her educational handout on the baptistery, "Like many things since Vatican II, the baptistery is still evolving" in shape, size, and location. "In its evolution since Vatican II, the font has been all over the church. Being able to see the font during the baptism was first thought [by liturgists] to be the critical issue. Now a consensus is forming [among liturgists] that visibility, while important, is a secondary issue. . . . You may have already guessed that the location of choice is becoming the entrance of the worship space. . . . Initially, when fonts were placed at the entrance, they were in the gathering space, or narthex. This has two drawbacks. The first drawback is that it really breaks up the flow of ritual when the entire body must move through doors to another space. Second, the gathering space is the place for random gathering, an important social experience. The nave, or main body of the church, is the place for ritual gathering, for the sacraments. When the font is placed up front, it says, 'Look but don't touch.' "[69]

Our pilgrim wonders why the baptismal font keeps changing, not only in placement but also in size and shape. Beginning sometime in the 1980s, liturgists moved to "return" to Baptism by full immersion, even though the Catholic Church never universally adopted such a practice, either in the ancient past or in the present. Even when John was baptizing in the Jordan, tradition holds that he poured water over the penitent's head rather than plunging him under. Likewise, the baptismal font is depicted in early Christian art as a shallow basin in which the baptized stood with feet immersed, while water was poured on him from a vase or large shell held by a priest.

Nevertheless, modern church designers and renovators produced a prototype vessel that would accommodate full-immersion Baptism, popularized by Baptist Protestants, who deny the validity of infant Baptism. The form that the font took in the 1980s and '90s is the bathtub, specifically the hot tub, sometimes known by the brand name Jacuzzi. Liturgical design consultant Fr. Andrew Ciferni, for instance, reminds Catholics that "the Romans built huge public baths where people gathered to do business or socialize while enjoying their own version of the hot tub."[70] This is the precedent he and other liturgists use for the design of fonts for new modern churches and for older churches remodeled into modern churches. Because the sacrament of Baptism represents both birth and death, large bodies of water are needed, he adds, because they bring to mind both life and death. "We can drown in

[69] Christine Reinhard, "The Baptismal Font," handout to parishioners of St. Francis Xavier Church in Petoskey, Michigan, 1999.

[70] Andrew D. Ciferni, "Environment for Catholic Worship: The Baptistery" (Federation of Diocesan Liturgical Commissions, 1988).

Modern church designers and renovators favor a prototype font that accommodates full-immersion Baptism, popularized by various Protestant sects that deny the validity of infant Baptism. The form the font took in the 1980s and '90s is the bathtub, specifically the hot tub.

the river that irrigates the fields or in the sea that provides fish for our tables."[71]

Our pilgrim, however, resents the size and shape of the baptismal font because it recalls, not life or death, but the hot-tub parties he attended when he was in college — something he would rather forget, or at least not be reminded of on his way to Mass. At the last modern church he visited, our pilgrim recalls, a bar of soap was floating in the Jacuzzi-like font, no doubt tossed in there by some eighth-grade prankster on his way to the weekly school

---

[71] Ibid.

Mass. No matter how much liturgists may want to imbue a certain object with a specific meaning, Catholics are inclined to determine on their own what they associate with any given form. If the associations are nearly always profane, the form of the sacred object fails to convey the symbolism that is intended.

Our pilgrim is also disturbed that the water in the baptismal font is flowing, which, via modern plumbing techniques, is supposed to recall the flowing waters of the Jordan. He knows from experience that this will be a distraction if not a terrible annoyance to him throughout the entire Mass. The sound of running water makes our pilgrim's bladder more active than he thinks is desirable.

Alas, the modern church baptismal font speaks little of the sacrament it's supposed to represent. There's no dove representing the Holy Spirit, no iconography of John the Baptist or the parting of the Red Sea. There's no sense of the struggle between good and evil, no artwork that conveys the fact that the sacrament of Baptism is truly death conquered by the saving power of Christ.

*The modern church's worship space
doesn't lift the soul to God*

Once through the doors leading into the modern church worship space, often called the "main worship space," our pilgrim realizes that there are no holy-water fonts for him to dip his fingers into to bless himself. Fortunately he recalls a priest at Mass in a new modern church once explaining to his congregation that the water of the baptismal pool is to be used as holy water "because that's what it is." In the modern church, he added, "everyone must dip into the same vessel as a sign of unity." Our pilgrim returns, then, to bless himself from the waters of the pool, wondering how the people entering the side doors nearer the parking lot ever bless themselves with holy water.

*There's no focal point in the modern "worship space." The altar is
too low to be visible, and the priest's chair, at the level of the congregation,
is inconspicuous to all but those sitting or standing in the first few rows.*

Ugly as Sin

The so-called main worship space doesn't seem different from the gathering space. The noise of the gathering chatter spills over into this next "space." It's no less light in here. His eyes needn't adjust. As he looks up, however, he's startled to see that he's nearly face-to-face with the altar. The priest is sitting in his "presider's chair" with his back to our pilgrim, surely not welcoming in the least.

Because our pilgrim is a few minutes late, the congregation can't help but be distracted by his entrance (and the entrance of other latecomers, somewhat chattier). He quickly moves off to the left, looking for a sign of the Blessed Sacrament so that he can make a proper genuflection as a sign of reverence to the Real Presence of Jesus.

Not finding any sign of the tabernacle, he takes a seat near the back of the circle. The seating surrounds the altar on three sides. There are no wooden pews, no kneelers — only cushioned seats that are so comfortable and casual that many in the congregation sit with their legs crossed and one arm stretched out over the back of the seat next to them. Others have their feet resting on the backs of the seats in front of them. Our pilgrim is a bit disconcerted by the casual posture — no doubt a result of the casual atmosphere of the modern church. He's used to praying before the Blessed Sacrament on his knees to prepare to celebrate the sacred mysteries, to be put in the proper frame of mind, to place himself in the presence of God. But his surroundings, least of all the chairs, he finds not at all conducive to prayer or reverence. There is nothing to raise his heart, his mind, and his soul to God.

He peers around at the bare walls. There's no sacred art save for some unidentifiable polychrome reliefs possibly made of pewter that are too far away for him to make out whether the images are of man or beast. There's whispering and quiet chatting among the congregation; some of the faithful are staring into the eyes of others who look back at them across the church.

Our pilgrim finds no natural focal point here. The altar is too low to be visible. The priest sitting down at the level of the congregation is inconspicuous as well, to all but the people sitting and standing in the first few rows.

Someone is reading from the letter of Paul to the Corinthians. Our pilgrim hears the voice from a nearby loudspeaker but can't find the pulpit or ambo. The eyes of those surrounding him offer no clue. Some are looking at the organ pipes, other at the choir members and the band who seem most prominent in this arrangement. Others have caught the eyes of relatives and friends. Raised eyebrows, nods of the head, and expressions of familiarity indicate casual hellos.

Our pilgrim is neither awed nor humbled here in the worship space of the people. He can sense, too, that no one else is awed or humbled. The casualness in dress and demeanor at the modern church is striking, surely a result of the casualness and informality of the modern church itself. Its proportions, too, are different from those of other churches. The relatively low ceilings give the worship space a horizontality you expect to find at home or in a restaurant. There are no arched windows, no columns, none of the familiar language elements that make up a church.

Perhaps most disconcerting for our pilgrim is that there's no sanctuary distinct from the nave. The main worship space apparently encompasses both areas of the traditional church. The body has been decapitated, the head subsumed. The modern church evokes a modern non-hierarchy: everything is equal. The worship space seems to dismiss Christ and the hierarchy of His Catholic Church. There are theaters and lecture halls, our pilgrim thinks, that give greater glory to God. In such a church, how many in the congregation have their minds lifted to the eternal? In such a place, how many manage to engage in true worship — in thanksgiving, adoration, reparation, and supplication? This is no sacred place, he concludes. It's a meeting space.

Ugly as Sin

⌒

Chairs promote comfort, not prayer and adoration

Throughout the Liturgy, there's no kneeling, only sitting and standing. Since there are no kneelers, local logic holds that kneeling is impossible. No one assumes the distinct posture for Catholic prayer, in adoration and humility. In this modern church, adoration is unheard of; humility is a thing for pious grandmothers who still attend downtown churches. Rather, in the modern church, our pilgrim assumes the "posture of celebration," which liturgists claim doesn't include kneeling.

Our pilgrim reflects that someone must misunderstand what *celebration* means. The Liturgy is "celebrated," but it isn't a celebration akin to a New Year's Eve party. *Celebrate* has a number of meanings. Its primary meaning, according to *Webster's New World Dictionary*, is "to perform (a ritual, ceremony, etc.) publicly and formally; solemnize." Its second sense is "to commemorate with ceremony." It's in these two senses that the celebration of the Mass has its meaning. Jesus did say, "Do this in memory of me." Accordingly, celebration of the Liturgy includes many parts with different aspects, e.g., praise, penance, adoration, etc. To ignore these aspects of the celebration is summarily to dismiss them. The richness and meaning of the Holy Sacrifice of the Mass is lost. Kneeling isn't a posture of celebration only if we're speaking of celebration in the sense of a party or festivity, which Holy Mass is not.

The portable stackable chairs used in the modern church are further justified on grounds of flexibility. According to liturgical consultants, such seating "allows the room and its furniture to serve the community rather than the community finding itself a slave to the immobility of the seating."[72] The various designs used

---

[72] Andrew D. Ciferni, "Environment for Catholic Worship: Assembly Seating and the Presider's Chair" (Federation of Diocesan Liturgical Commissions, 1988).

Seating in the modern church is often made up of either portable cushioned chairs or pews without kneelers, or a combination of both.

to promote flexibility seem to be ways to redefine the whole Catholic church building, on the model of a secular or profane building, one that isn't set aside for sacred purposes.

At Christ the King Church in Las Vegas, the worship space is reconfigured every few months. Sometimes the altar is in the center of the square building; at other times it's against one wall or another. Sometimes the chairs are arranged encircling the altar; sometimes they're configured on three sides in a fan shape or on two sides in an antiphonal configuration. When parishioners arrive for Mass there, they don't know what to expect. The sense of permanence that they have long come to expect from a church has been injured. Whatever the configuration, however, the modern church is never designed in a basilican arrangement with chairs all facing one direction; that's considered too clerical, too hierarchical.

⌒

The modern church's lectern
competes with the altar

If our pilgrim visits an older renovated church, such as St. Francis Xavier Church in Petoskey, Michigan, he might notice that the elevated pulpit, sometimes with iconographic carvings, has been removed and replaced by a lectern that the liturgists call an ambo, the terminology used in first-millennium churches, despite the fact that these modern secular lecterns — many of which look as if they belong in a college lecture hall or a banquet room — bear little resemblance to the ancient stone ambos with steps leading up both sides to accommodate the priest and his acolytes.

Just as the baptismal font has jumped around the church, so has the lectern, our pilgrim finds. In churches designed in the late '60s or '70s, the lectern was often placed side by side with the altar — neither was centered in the sanctuary — to manifest the latest liturgical theory that equated in importance and magnitude the Liturgy of the Word and Liturgy of the Eucharist. In other modern churches, the lectern was placed directly in front of the altar, and both were centered in the sanctuary. According to liturgists and church designers, this was done humbly to admit Catholics' "past failure to balance the proclamation of God's Word with our traditional emphasis on the celebration of the Sacraments."[73] Often the lectern is made of the same wood as the altar. It's often vested or covered with a linen hanging just like the altar. Candles are sometimes placed near the lectern, just as candles are required on or near the altar. As a result, our pilgrim notices that the altar is diminished in its proper importance and actually has to compete with the lectern to be the focal point of the sanctuary and church.

In a 1980s or '90s modern church, our pilgrim might find the lectern anywhere. At some point in the '80s, the monastic antiphonal arrangement was introduced as an innovation to parishes. The antiphonal modern church, such as Our Lady of Mt. Carmel in Newport News, Virginia, is configured with an altar at one end of the building and the lectern at the other, both in a central aisle. Seating is on two sides of the aisle, with seats facing the aisle and each other. In the late '90s, the lectern became a wild card. Now anything goes.

⟶

The modern church's music ministry
competes with holy Mass

The modern church accommodates a cantor, a choir, and a band in a prominent spot. A pianist, a drummer, a guitarist, a bass player, several woodwind players, and the choir are situated

---

[73] Andrew D. Ciferni, "Environment for Catholic Worship: The Ambo" (Federation of Diocesan Liturgical Commissions, 1988).

*One of the fashions of recent decades is to place the lectern
side by side with the altar — neither one centered in the sanctuary —
to manifest the inaccurate liturgical theory that equates in importance
and magnitude the Liturgy of the Word and the Liturgy of the Eucharist.*

conspicuously up front, facing the congregation. Our pilgrim notices the "music ministry" more so than he notices the altar or the lectern — both visibly and audibly. They seem to him a performance group that doesn't lead the congregation in song as much as it plays tunes for their edification. (The choir loft is a taboo in the modern church. According to liturgists, Catholics are "so accustomed to choir lofts in the rear of the nave that we fail to reflect on the fact that God could have turned our ears around if we were supposed to hear music from behind!"[74])

The songs that are hammered out by the band and choir, with the exception of "On Eagle's Wings," are unknown to our pilgrim and, apparently, judging from their silence, to most others seated nearby. The modern church, with its attributes of coziness and folksiness, demands music that is cozy and folksy. When singing the Lord's Prayer, our pilgrim reluctantly joins in with the congregation, holding hands with those seated next to him, but because of the mustard-yellow carpeting, he hears only himself singing, as if he's the only one present at the Liturgy, as if he's holding his hands out to no one. The carpeting, an impermanent flooring to be sure, absorbs the voices that ought to resound. The noise of the instrumentalists also militates against hearing anything chanted or sung in the modern church.

During the responsorial psalm, our pilgrim is taken aback when the cantor stands in front of the altar and the lectern, with microphone in hand to belt out a tune in her beautiful sing-the-Blues voice. He's so distracted by the soloist in the white gown that he's unable to pray; he's unable to prepare for hearing the Gospel preached, for witnessing the Holy Sacrifice, or for receiving the Body, Blood, soul, and divinity of Christ in full communion with

---

[74] Andrew D. Ciferni, "Environment for Catholic Worship: Musical Instruments" (Federation of Diocesan Liturgical Commissions, 1988).

the universal Church. In other words, he finds it difficult to participate actively in the Liturgy. In fact, he finds it difficult to participate in *any* meaningful way — actively or passively. If this modern church weren't set up in a theater-like arrangement, our pilgrim reflects, it wouldn't encourage such theatricality in the Liturgy.

⌒

*The modern church's images don't
teach the Faith or evangelize*

When our pilgrim's eyes wander to settle on an inspiring mural or devotional shrine, he's again frustrated with the modern church. Although the sacred image or icon has always been an important part of the Catholic church building, the modern church is typically not amenable to statues, painted icons, frescoes, mosaics, or any other portrayal that would be considered too overt a manifestation of the Christian Faith. Liturgists say that in the modern church, sacred images of any sort can distract the pilgrim from the liturgical actions and that, if they're permanent fixtures, the worship space might be seen exclusively as a sacred space. Consequently, there are no side-aisle shrines, no stained-glass windows, no crucifixes to contemplate, no meaningful iconography whatsoever to lift man's mind away from his everyday thoughts.

Still, our pilgrim does spot a few wall hangings that create a spark of color on the otherwise barren walls. If the subjects are re-ligious in nature, their presentation renders the subjects wholly unrecognizable.

Our pilgrim also sees that small bare crosses placed at different angles throughout a section of this modern church serve as the Stations of the Cross. One of the fads of the 1990s modern church was to include temporary multicultural works of art and symbols, such as the yin-yang, that are recognizable for their "universality." The modern church avoids conveying specifically Christian meaning to anyone; these universal symbols and multicultural works don't speak much to the Christian West. Some aren't properly multicultural or universal, in that they're simply meaningless, like the curtain-like sculpture hanging above the altar in St. John's Church in West Chester, Ohio, or the puffy clouds floating lifelessly in the sanctuary of the renovated St. Vivian's Church in Cincinnati.

Another noteworthy 1990s trend was that of depicting in quasisacred works of art "contemporary role models" or "baptismal witnesses" instead of canonized saints. Since they're contemporary, these role models can be changed with the times, just as the photos of sports stars on the wall of a diner might change from decade to decade: Yogi Berra and Joe DiMaggio in the 1950s to Tiger Woods and Sammy Sosa in the 1990s. These images are ephemeral and based on the changing tastes of the people, unlike images of the saints, which serve as timeless reminders of living the Christian life. Here our pilgrim discovers that the wall hangings depict Martin Luther King, Karl Rahner, Dr. Tom Dooley, and Sr. Thea Bowman.

Depicting contemporary role models — whether Catholic or non-Catholic — undermines the artistic tradition and theology of the sacred image by providing a "profane" icon. When the modern church designer or renovator chooses to depict the profane, he aligns himself with the ancient Iconoclasts, who broke with the authentic tradition of the Church by forbidding representations of Christ and religious images in general. In fact, Pope John Paul II addressed this issue in his 1987 apostolic letter *Duodecimum saeculum*, and again in his 1999 "Letter to Artists," when he wrote that the Iconoclasts, "not without contradiction or ambiguity . . . allowed profane images, in particular those of the emperor with the signs of reverence that were attached to them."

Thus, while, in furnishings such as a crucifix or the Stations of the Cross, the modern church gives minimal traditional expression

A few wall hangings, such as these Stations of the Cross, create a spark of color on the otherwise barren wall paneling.

to the sacred, it displays profane wall hangings as sacred icons, yet without traditional content. The ancient theology of the icon is that a sacred image points beyond itself to a spiritual reality (e.g., the Annunciation, the Incarnation, the presentation of the Sacred Heart to St. Margaret Mary Alacoque) on which the pilgrim meditates. It brings his mind into harmony with God. Catholics do this properly through veneration. In the words of St. Thomas Aquinas, "the honor rendered to an image passes to its prototype," and "whoever venerates an image venerates the person portrayed in it."[75] Thus, if the profane icon is venerated, the "role model"

[75] *Catechism of the Catholic Church*, no. 2132.

A renovation of St. Robert Bellarmine Church in Cincinnati replaced the
sanctuary crucifix with an "Icon of Seasons." Designed by renowned artist
William J. Schickel, this tapestry holder displays what he calls "seasonal
works of art," depicting a glowing sun, flying birds, and swaying wheat.
Although this piece of art is said to be a standing processional cross, it takes
the form of a framed rectangle. The structure is composed of two intersecting
pieces of wood, yet four multicolored square cloths obscure the cruciform.
To the pilgrim, it simply looks like a square four-paneled painting. The
cross is so obscured, so inconspicuous, that it isn't recognizable as such.

himself is venerated. As such, the modern church presents a disordered understanding of the Communion of the Saints. Most likely, however, the profane icon won't be venerated any more than will a photo of Marilyn Monroe or Frank Sinatra hanging on the wall of a diner. But unlike Marilyn and Frank, the role-model reliefs or wall hangings will almost always require a plaque identifying the person depicted.

Our pilgrim notices how bright it is in the modern church. Since the worship space isn't glazed with stained glass, the external light isn't transformed into multicolored patterns, but simply floods through the few transparent windows, giving the worship space a warm, sunny feel.

Our pilgrim is fortunate, because some modern churches have no windows at all. The flood of light in those churches comes only from hanging or recessed fluorescent fixtures. Stained glass, especially depicting narratives from Scripture or from the lives of the saints, are too ecclesiastical, too "churchy" for the modern church.

While still in the bright worship space, our pilgrim can barely make out an image of seven silhouetted figures on the wall who appear to be ascending a mountain at sunset. The image hangs above and behind the altar on a white projection screen throughout the pastor's homily. At the end of his sermon, the lights dim and mechanical shades noisily descend over the windows. The band begins to play some soft, soothing background music as the hiking image becomes animated. The seven hikers climb easily to the top of the hill, whereupon the sun sets and the sky is illumined only by the rays of a crescent moon. This, our pilgrim concludes, is art in the modern church: fleeting and uninspiring, devoid of any real meaning beyond what is imputed to it by each of the faithful.

The lights are brightened, and the shades are lifted by unseen mechanical pulleys.

⁓

The modern church has no crucifix
to remind us of Christ's redemptive Sacrifice

During the Eucharistic Prayer, as the priest, with his arms outstretched, pronounces the words of consecration, our pilgrim glances about a while standing in the posture of celebration with the rest of the congregation — hoping his eyes will come to rest on a crucifix. He's accustomed to contemplating the Incarnation via the visible symbol of the Cross with the corpus of Jesus. He's accustomed to meditating on the suffering that Christ endured on the Cross by seeing His visible wounds; he's accustomed to venerating the crucifix as a symbol of Christ's redemption of man through this great Sacrifice. The crucifix reminds our pilgrim that it is this redemptive sacrifice that's being re-presented through the Holy Sacrifice of the Mass by the hands of the ordained priest.

In this modern church, however, our pilgrim finds no crucifix with the corpus of Jesus. While craning his neck, he spies only a bare plus sign set on a metal pole that stands near the altar. Halfway through the prayer of consecration, our pilgrim realizes that this plus sign is a representation of the Greek cross. It's nothing to contemplate, he thinks; it doesn't exactly help him participate in the Holy Sacrifice. This piece of "sacred art" is another ephemeral symbol. At the beginning of Mass, the cross-bearer carried in this processional cross; and during the recessional hymn, as the band plays their grand finale, the cross-bearer will take up the cross and store it in the sacristy, sight unseen, until the next Saturday afternoon.

The design of the modern processional cross isn't always as straightforward as the simple Greek plus sign. It may have concentric circles radiating from its intersection or a grillwork superimposed on it; there may be a circular opening at its center or the image of a towel draped over the horizontal bar.

The crucifix in the modern church isn't always as straightforward and simple as is the popular barren Greek plus sign.

⌒

The modern church's altar is only one
among many focal points of attention

The altar of the modern church is placed in the midst of the congregation, raised on a one-step platform, not too high as not to make it too prominent a furnishing. It's made of wood with four legs, much like a table. Since there's no stone slab, there's no ref-erence to Christ the Cornerstone; there's no reference to sacrifice. Since there are no relics interred in the wooden altar (called a "holy table" in modern church parlance), there's no reference to the sacrifice of the martyrs.

The holy table isn't a fixed furnishing. Often it moves with the season. The doctrine of liturgical flexibility necessitates that the holy table, along with the lectern, be portable, just like all other furnishings in the modern church. In fact, the holy table can even be removed to the sacristy when it's necessary for the modern church to be used for modern liturgical performances or meetings.

The arrangement of the modern church makes it such that the holy table isn't so much the focus of the worship space as much as it's one of the focal points, the others being the presider's chair (where the priest sits or stands during most of the Liturgy), the lectern, the choir and band, and even other members of the congregation. (According to the liturgist, "the assembly itself . . . is the primary symbol of Christ's presence . . . in our places of worship."[76]) The holy table becomes the focal point of the modern church only when the priest recites the Eucharistic Prayer, and even then our pilgrim's attention is divided between altar and assembly.

[76] Andrew D. Ciferni, "Environment for Catholic Worship: The Altar" (Federation of Diocesan Liturgical Commissions, 1988).

Furthermore, our pilgrim notes, all traces of the sacrificial aspect of the Mass are removed. First, there's no indication that the table is an altar: it isn't made of stone; it resembles a dining table and often isn't vested in altar linens. With the congregation gathered around the holy table, the Lord's Supper, a banquet, is overly emphasized so as to overshadow any sacrificial nature of the ritual. Second, there's no sacrificial iconography, not even a crucifix.

Our pilgrim can barely see the altar or the priest. Standing at his seat in the back of the circle of chairs, he finds it hard to think of sacrifice. Nor does this church help him reflect on the Last Supper, at which Jesus instituted the Holy Eucharist. The Eucharistic Prayer has become just another prayer of the Mass.

In older renovated churches, a similar desacralizing has taken place. The old stone altar along with its decorative baldacchino or

The holy table overshadows the Sacrifice.

*The holy table is just one among many finely crafted
new furnishings, carefully matched by the interior designer.*

reredos have been dismantled and removed. A new holy table, made of wood, has been built to resemble the lectern and the presider's chair and placed out in the midst of the congregation, eliminating the sanctuary and any thoughts of sacrifice. The altar now sits so low in the church building that few can see it from their seat. Ultimately, the holy table is just one among many finely crafted new furnishings, carefully matched by an interior designer.

At Communion time, numerous lay distributors approach the altar to retrieve sacred Hosts. One by one, they peel away from altar and priest to take up their assigned positions in the modern church. Since there's no central aisle, our pilgrim is confused. Communion distributors stand in so many spots that it's difficult for him to know whom he's supposed to approach. The man on his left heads left toward one aisle. The woman on his right moves to her right toward another aisle. There's little sense that he's receiving Communion in unity with this particular congregation, let alone in *communio* with the universal Church. Most of the congregation don't receive the Sacred Body and Blood of Jesus near the altar or even within sight of the altar.

In other words, because of the arrangement of the modern church, Holy Communion is carried out with little or no reference to the sacrificial altar.

⌒

The tabernacle is absent, as is Christ
from the modern church

When the Mass has ended and the cross-bearer carries the portable Greek cross out of the worship space, processing with the priest, the assembly files out of the rows after him, rushing toward the gathering area, chatting, waving, hugging, and guffawing. In a few moments, our pilgrim is left sitting alone in the empty modern church worship space, with bulletins left behind on the seats and on the floor. There's a feeling of barrenness and loneliness all around, as if he had attended a baseball game and stayed behind in the stadium after the game, after all the players had left the field and after the fans had filed out to the parking lot — a vast emptiness.

The worship space seems to our pilgrim a dead space, a place of no-place — a result of the building's transgressions of the natural laws of church architecture. So he, too, heads back toward the gathering space, determined to find where the Blessed Sacrament is reserved. Once through the doors, he looks about to see hallways, doors to offices, drinking fountains, and phones. Walking up to a coffee and doughnut stand that had apparently been assembled in the gathering space while he was at Mass, he first asks a middle-age man where he can find the tabernacle. The man shrugs, unable to help. He next asks an older woman where the priest reserves the Blessed Sacrament. "Hmm. That's a good question," she responds cheerfully. "I don't know."

Thus, our pilgrim embarks by himself on a search for what the modern church designer calls the "eucharistic chapel" or "eucharistic sector." He makes his way through the crowd of people who just a few moments before were the assembly of the worship space. Now they have become the primary furnishings of the gathering space. Down one of the hallways he sees a sign on a closed door that reads, "Reconciliation Chapel. 4:00-4:30, Saturdays."

Curious, he pushes open the door.

A small but brightly lit room is beyond. There are a few abstract wall hangings decorating one wall, two seats, and a couch. How many parishioners who attend this modern church, our

Inconspicuous doors in the wall lead to the Reconciliation chapel.

pilgrim wonders, even know this "chapel" is here? Its inconspicuousness makes it a poor sign for the sacrament of Penance. If our pilgrim had not seen the sign that read "Reconciliation Chapel," he never could have guessed the function of the room.

Further down the hallway is a set of locked glass doors. Looking in, our pilgrim sees a small altar table set in the middle of a tiny office space. Ten chairs are lined up in one row on either side of the altar, and a lectern stands at the other end of the office. The sign on this door reads, "Day Chapel: Daily worship, Monday-Friday, 11:00 a.m."

As our pilgrim continues down the hallway, he passes the restrooms and a large bulletin board with postings about what's happening in the parish that month. At the end of the hallway is an open doorway. Here in the center of a small square room the tabernacle sits on a thin column. Four chairs, one facing each side of the tabernacle, are set up with kneeling cushions placed in front. Although the din from the gathering space reaches the eucharistic chapel, there's no one but our pilgrim here, who kneels to give thanks in adoration for a few moments before returning to his car.

Set on its column, this tabernacle resembles a bird feeder more than anything else, our pilgrim thinks. But this isn't always the case. Some modern church tabernacles aren't set on pillars but

Sometimes directions are posted so that worshipers can find Jesus in the Blessed Sacrament.

THE EUCHARIST IS RESERVED IN THE SMALL CHAPEL AT THE FRONT OF THE MAIN CHAPEL ON THE RIGHT SIDE

A tabernacle resembling a bird feeder is set on
a pillar (left). The modern "sacrament tower"
can resemble a tall, slender fish tank (right).

appear as tall rectangular, cylindrical, or conical structures known as "sacrament towers." The tower designed by James Postell at St. Charles Borromeo Church in Kettering, Ohio, is made of glass and wood.[77] It looks like a tall, slender fish tank or aquarium. With the

---

[77] According to the *Code of Canon Law*, "The tabernacle into which the Eucharist is regularly reserved is to be immovable, made of solid and opaque material, and locked so that the danger of profanation may be entirely avoided" (can. 938.3).

The eucharistic chapel is set apart
from the rest of the church.

transparent glazing, a pilgrim there can see hundreds of consecrated hosts piled up inside.

Once finished with his prayer of thanksgiving, our pilgrim re-
treats down the hall, through the gathering space, and out into the
sea of cars in the parking lot, many of which are still struggling to
get away from this modern church until next Saturday afternoon.

A rear entrance to this church leads to the obscure eucharistic chapel.

Chapter Four

Why modern architects secularized our churches
(or, bad theology has done
more damage than bad taste)

If the modern church building is the source of so much frustration, confusion, and consternation for our pious pilgrim, how and *why* did it come into being? Since the common man — Catholic or not — experiences the modern church as banal and uninspiring, why do parishes continue to build such edifices?

Creators of these banal structures often justify their work by appealing to the Second Vatican Council, a meeting of the world's bishops to discuss the current state of the Church at that time and to recommend a pastoral course to follow in the twenty-first century.

When the bishops met in Rome from 1962 to 1965, the Church's patrimony of sacred architecture was rich. The universal Church was blessed with beautiful churches that gave glory to God and were conducive to public worship and private devotion. Catholic churches, even the most modest of structures, could be readily identified for what they were. Most lay Catholics had at least a passing familiarity with the churches of past decades and centuries. They appreciated the other-worldly feel of their interiors, the familiar signs of the spire and bell tower, statues and stained glass, pews and crucifix, high altar and tabernacle, pulpit and confessional. When they walked past one of these houses of God, they knew well that inside they would find sanctuary from the busy outside world, respite from the profane, and a quiet and prayerful atmosphere in which they could meet God in a unique way: through Holy Mass, adoration of the Blessed Sacrament, and various devotions. These churches were understood as sacred places where you could stand with the angels and saints, adoring Christ and honoring His Blessed Mother.

Such sacred places still made visible the Church there amid the world. Its spire or dome surmounted by the cross contrasted with the varying forms of secular buildings in most places, and its bell tower was a welcome sign to pilgrims and tourists, locals and merchants. Its bells resounding through the city square or the neighboring farmland served as both a timepiece and a call to prayer. In short, the church was a recognizable structure, its function well known. It was a sacred place conducive to worship, to intercessory prayer, a place where you could repent, confess, and reconcile. This was the common understanding of a church building as the council fathers gathered to discuss *Sacrosanctum Concilium*, the Constitution on the Sacred Liturgy, the first document of the Council, promulgated by Pope Paul VI in 1963.

Although most Catholics in the pews wouldn't even know of the existence of *Sacrosanctum Concilium* until years or even decades later, this document was used to justify the reform of Catholic church architecture in the years immediately following the council. It's an understatement to say that *Sacrosanctum Concilium* was falsely used as the catalyst for such a reformation.

Even well before the council, churches of previous centuries had been deemed "irrelevant" by certain Church liturgists who were more interested in the innovative architectural theories that produced much of the twentieth century's stark, minimalist public architecture. Traditional architectural elements and furnishings were disparaged, and a new model was born, based on architectural Modernism with its divorce from traditional models, its cold, hard lines, and its overemphasis on utility.

The postwar building boom saw the construction of numerous Catholic churches as parishes grew and the Church greatly increased in numbers throughout North America. The churches built in this brief era were diverse in design, but some were obviously disconnected with the tradition of Catholic architecture, reflecting a Protestant or secular influence. Some of these new churches built before the council were designed as hulking masses in the shape of seashells, sailboats, arks, and other nautical themes; rocket ships, beehives, tepees, lunar landing pods, and various shapes of origami — forms that would become more common and no less ugly in later decades.

Designers of these ugly churches capitalized on the spirit of change that swept through Western society during the tumultuous '60s. They claimed the spirit of Vatican II as their justification for the reformation of church architecture. No longer were they limited to constructing new experimental churches in the few places where they were welcomed; they found that they could even successfully invoke the council to advocate the structural reform of existing churches. It made selling both their renovation and new building design ideas much easier. In other words, they used the council to legitimize the experimental church designs that the common people had consistently rejected.

At a time when the council documents were rarely consulted and not readily available, the laity were willing to put their trust in these authorities, whom they expected to have the best interests of the Church at heart. If a pastor, a bishop, or a priest-liturgist explained to parishioners that their church building *had to change* or that a new stark, uninspiring church was *required*, the laity accepted it — begrudgingly perhaps — because such plans were said to be predicated on directives from the council fathers. Proponents

*The postwar building boom saw the construction of
numerous Catholic churches as parishes grew and the Church
greatly increased in numbers throughout North America.
The churches built in this brief era were diverse in design, but some
were obviously disconnected with the tradition of Catholic architecture.*

*New churches being built in Europe similarly
broke with Catholic architectural tradition.*

of this new architecture took great liberties with the council documents, and little was called into question.

Many of the changes in church architecture, for instance, were said to be predicated on *Sacrosanctum Concilium*'s idea of promoting "active participation" in the Liturgy. In fact, many beautiful churches were destroyed in the name of active participation; many uninspiring and ugly edifices were erected under the same pretense. In older churches, under the pretense of fostering active participation, the altars were often moved into the midst of the people, causing the disfigurement of their former sanctuaries. In the name of active participation, statues, tabernacle, high altars with beautiful reredos structures, communion rails, baldacchinos, and aisle shrines were removed; murals and mosaics were whitewashed or covered with paneling — all because these things were said to distract people from active participation in the Mass. This line of reasoning reached the height of absurdity when, a few years later, pews were ripped out. They, too, were a kind of distraction, and all that kneeling was said to be misplaced and impeded active participation — the ideal supposedly set forth by the Second Vatican Council. Active participation, however, was simply an abused concept.[78] It was used to justify some of the radical theories that are still being promoted widely at the dawn of the twenty-first century.

Commenting on this abuse, Abbot Boniface Luykx, one of the council fathers who helped draft *Sacrosanctum Concilium*, explained that renovators "destroyed many good churches — beautiful churches — in the name of [active participation of] the

[78] The term *active participation* is still widely misunderstood to this day. The official Latin version uses the term *actuosa participatio*. The term *actuosa* incorporates both the contemplative (internal) and active (external) aspects of participation. *Activa*, which also means "active," normally excludes the contemplative aspect. The choice of *actuosa* instead of *activa* is significant.

people. When they threw the altar in the midst of the church, they destroyed beautiful altar rails and structures of the church that were oriented towards the altar and the apse. So they destroyed the inner logic and dynamics of many churches because of a misunderstood principle."[79]

⌒

Vatican II called for preservation of our churches

Sacrosanctum Concilium was the only document that addressed the question of art in our churches. Nevertheless, this document didn't use the word *architecture* even once. That's because the council had precious little to say about the reform of Catholic church architecture. The changes that were promoted in parishes couldn't have been based on council mandates. Rather, the new church designs were justified by subjective opinions rooted in current architectural theories and innovative liturgical ideas that had never been officially adopted by the Catholic Church.

Far from advocating the reform of church architecture, *Sacrosanctum Concilium* actually called for the preservation of sacred art and furnishings in the Church's sacred places. One of the most significant statements of the section dealing with this issue came in paragraph 123: "In the course of the centuries [the Church] has brought into being a treasury of art which must be carefully preserved." Bishops were warned that they "must be very careful to see that sacred furnishings and works of value are not disposed of or allowed to deteriorate; for they are the house of God."[80]

Yet the rearrangement and denuding of traditional churches in the late 1960s and early '70s proves that these statements were little heeded in Christendom. The blatant disregard for these

---

[79] Abbot Boniface Luykx, "Liturgical Architecture: *Domus Dei* or *Domus Ecclesiae?*" *Catholic Dossier* (May-June 1997).

[80] *Sacrosanctum Concilium*, no. 126.

In the name of "active participation," high altars were removed from churches by brute force and jackhammers.

mandates became so common that in 1971 the Vatican reiterated its warning to the bishops in a short document on the care and preservation of the Church's historical and artistic patrimony, *Opera Artis*:

> Disregarding the warnings and legislation of the Holy See, many people have made unwarranted changes in places of worship under the pretext of carrying out the reform of the Liturgy and thus have caused the disfigurement or loss of priceless works of art. Mindful of the legislation of Vatican Council II and of the directives in the documents of the Holy See, bishops are to exercise unfailing vigilance to ensure that the remodeling of places of worship by reason of the reform of the Liturgy is carried out with utmost caution.[81]

Nevertheless, church renovators of the 1970s and thereafter steered their own course and continued to do so falsely in the name of the Second Vatican Council and the reformed Liturgy (with which a great many liberties were being taken as well).

At the dawn of the twenty-first century, Archbishop Rembert Weakland of Milwaukee oversaw the denuding of his cathedral church even after receiving in writing a warning directed to him personally by Vatican officials. The primary artistic element of the old Milwaukee cathedral was an ornate forty-foot-high baldacchino, a marble canopy built over the high altar, which was dismissed by the archbishop as having "no artistic or historic value."[82] Archbishop Weakland had the baldacchino dismantled and removed.

[81] *Opera Artis*, Circular Letter on the Care of the Church's Historical and Artistic Heritage, Sacred Congregation for the Clergy, approved by Pope Paul VI, 1971.

[82] Letter from Archbishop Rembert G. Weakland to priests, deacons, and parish administrators in the Archdiocese of Milwaukee, July 5, 2001.

Milwaukee's Archbishop Rembert Weakland oversaw the denuding of his cathedral even after receiving in writing a warning directed to him by Vatican officials. The primary artistic element of the old cathedral was this ornate forty-foot-high marble dome baldacchino, which Weakland dismissed as having "no artistic or historic value." He had it dismantled and removed.

Ugly as Sin

⌒

Fashion has always threatened church architecture

If today Catholics can so easily see — albeit with hindsight of four decades or so — that the council did nothing to promote modern architectural changes but actually required the preservation of the Church's sacred patrimony, why did the church designers and renovators press on with their illicit activities?

The fact is that ever since Christians have established holy places for sacred worship, there have been those who sought either to destroy these houses of God or to convert them for pagan or secular purposes. Throughout the centuries and for a multitude of reasons, churches have been prime targets for barbarians, reformers, and revolutionaries. Beginning with the sack of Rome by the Visigoths in 410 and continuing to present-day China, where the Communist government has promoted church destruction, various anti-Christian factions have sought to eliminate the Church by destroying her architectural patrimony, the centers of Catholic worship and the heart of Christian communities.

During the era of the Protestant Reformation especially, the patrimony of the Church, i.e., her buildings, furnishings, sacred vestments and vessels, and works of sacred art, suffered dearly as a result of ideological, theological, and political disputes. The fracturing of the Catholic Church produced a wave of violence that wreaked not only indiscriminate damage, but also sacrilegious destruction. When, for instance, King Henry VIII severed ties with the Pope and created the Church of England, 376 English monasteries were confiscated, looted, and then sacked by the politician Thomas Cromwell and his men. All of the sacred furnishings were ripped out. These works of sacred art no longer gave glory to God but condemned their thieves for sacrilege. Most of the monasteries were then demolished with gunpowder. The English landscape became disfigured and looked as though it had been ravaged by barbarians.

A group of Catholics holding a prayer vigil in front of the Cathedral Basilica of the Assumption in Covington, Kentucky, because it was slated for renovation. In recent years, many lay Catholics have come to fear news that their churches will be remodeled and have joined together in growing numbers to oppose renovations that violate the natural laws of church architecture.

At the same time, the Calvinist movement was spreading throughout rural France, Holland, and Belgium. Supported by European princes eager to throw off the moral constraints of Catholicism, the Calvinists were intensely militant, sacking Catholic churches and monasteries wherever the movement settled.

Two hundred years later, a new anti-Catholic crusade gripped France. The French Revolution was ignited in 1789 by anti-monarchical intellectuals who upheld the principles of Liberalism: the beliefs that man is responsible to no authority, that man owes nothing to God, and that the mind and will of man is supreme.

*When King Henry VIII severed ties with the Pope and
created the Church of England, 376 monasteries were
confiscated, looted, and sacked. The English landscape became
disfigured and looked as if it had been ravaged by barbarians.*

Imagine, then, how they must have regarded sacred places of
worship.

The exclusive use of consecrated buildings for religious services was prohibited by the anticlerical government. By 1791,
Notre Dame was being used not only for ecclesiastical functions,
but for civic functions as well. When German troops threatened
France, the churches' religious goods were confiscated to aid the
military cause. Sacred vessels, church bells, choir grilles, bronze
tombs, and monuments were all carted away to be melted down
into cannonballs. Even one of Notre Dame's enormous bells was
taken in this wave of plundering.

Why modern architects secularized our churches

When Robespierre assumed the dictatorship of France and established what is now known as the Reign of Terror, one of his first acts was to outlaw all worship of the true God. In 1793, he established a new religion emanating from his own Deistic[83] convictions. This short-lived cult centered on a "Supreme Being" and was intended to add a spiritual component to the otherwise godless principles of the French Revolution. The new religion necessitated that Catholic churches be pruned of all Christian imagery. The buildings were converted into temples honoring the Supreme Being (the goddess Reason) or into museums or other buildings used for secular purposes.

Thousands of religious statues throughout France were indiscriminately destroyed. At Notre Dame, every statue on the Western façade, for instance, was plucked from its niche and smashed in the streets or thrown into the Seine.

Just decades later, in 1831, Victor Hugo's *Hunchback of Notre Dame* was published in France. One remarkable claim that the young writer made during his elaborate description of the architecture of the cathedral is that despite the grave damage that Notre Dame suffered at the hands of these revolutionaries, "fashion" had wrought the greater destruction. He drew up a list of his criticisms: the colored stained-glass windows had been removed, the interior was whitewashed, the tower over the central part of the cathedral was ripped off, the shape of the central entrance to the cathedral was deformed, and the chapels were filled with ugly decorations.

Hugo said that the ruin of Notre Dame was precipitated by three major forces:

[83] Deism is the belief in the existence of a God on purely rational grounds while denying revelation and authority. Its defining doctrine is that this God, or Supreme Being, created the world and its natural laws only to abandon them.

• *Time*, which "has gradually made deficiencies here and there, and has gnawed over its whole surface";

• "*Violence, brutalities, contusions, fractures* — these are the works of revolutions." This is the type of destruction, wrote Hugo, wrought by indiscriminate revolutionary violence;

• *Fashion*, which, Hugo claimed, has done more mischief than revolutions: "It has cut to the quick — it has attacked the very bone and framework of the art."

Hugo expressed his sorrow and indignation at the "numberless degradations and mutilations" that the hand of man had inflicted upon the venerable monument in the name of fashion, *not* revolution. "Upon the face of this old queen of the French cathedrals beside each wrinkle we constantly find a scar," wrote Hugo. "*Tempus edax, homo edacior.* Which we would willingly render thus: Time is blind, but man is stupid."[84]

Hugo observed that time and revolution devastated the edifice "with impartiality and grandeur." Yet fashion was perpetrated by "school-trained architects, licensed, privileged, and patented, degrading with all the discernment and selection of bad taste."[85] Thus, Hugo claimed that the worst destruction was perpetrated not by the atheistic Iconoclasts of the bloody French Revolution, as many historians would have it, but by these school-trained architects, slaves to bad taste. Hugo accused these men who assume the character of the architect of willful destruction, perversion, and re-creation, all in the name of fashion.

Considering all the damage wreaked by barbarians, reformers, and revolutionaries throughout the centuries, it's astounding to consider that slaves to fashion could bear more responsibility for

[84] Hugo, *The Hunchback of Notre Dame*, 133.
[85] Ibid.

the destruction of God's houses throughout Christendom. Without a doubt, Hugo's hypothesis bears out in the latter half of the twentieth century. The church designers and renovators of our time are submissive not only to fashions of art and architecture, but even more so to those of theology and ideology that underpin the fashions of liturgical architecture.

The modern equivalent to Hugo's "school-trained architects" appears in the character of a relatively new church professional known as the "liturgical design consultant" (LDC). Despite the fact that the Church has built beautiful edifices to the greater glory of God in *every* age without the aid of such consultants, these professionals are now commonly hired and, in many places, *required!*

These consultants have not only reordered traditional churches to reflect the latest liturgical and theological fashions, but they have also given the world Catholic churches that are, as we say in the colloquial, ugly as sin, as well as those that just don't look like churches.

⌒

Protestant theology has tainted
modern Catholic church architecture

Aiding the new LDCs was a controversial document entitled *Environment and Art in Catholic Worship* (EACW). A document of little authority but of massive application, EACW was released in 1978 as a provisional draft statement by the U.S. Bishops' Committee on Liturgy (BCL) under the leadership of San Francisco's Archbishop John Quinn. Yet the bishops' committee improperly issued EACW in the name of the National Conference of Catholic Bishops, implying the tacit approval of the Holy See.

"It would have been very helpful for all sorts of parishioners and countless parish committees over the past two decades to know that EACW had no juridically binding or obligatory force," wrote Msgr. William Smith in 1998, twenty years after the release of the document which quickly became the LDC's design and renovation manifesto.[86] Yet only in the late 1990s did the man in the pew come to understand that EACW is *not* a set of specific directives ratified by the U.S. bishops to be used when churches are designed or renovated.

Notre Dame professor and architect Duncan Stroik described EACW as "a document of architectural reductionism that reflects a liturgical reductionism. It's fearful of symbols, complexity, history, art, and even architecture."[87] Canonist Duane L. C. M. Galles outlined the extent of its usage to justify objectionable changes during the renovation process:

> Since 1978 not a few dioceses adopted EACW's recommendations as a set of "directives" to be employed during the renovation of existing churches as well as in the design and construction of new ones. EACW is cited as the authority for the sometimes drastic changes such as destruction of communion rails, ripping out of high altars and replacing them with "tables" in the center of the church building, moving the reserved Blessed Sacrament out of the sanctuary, etc. . . .
>
> The following assertion made by the administrator of a parish in the Archdiocese of Cincinnati is typical: "Many who object to the design do not realize that the Church has given rather specific directives for Catholic worship space. The National Conference of Catholic Bishops has published 'Environment and Art in Catholic Worship.' If major repair work is to be done, this authoritative teaching from the Bishops has to be a guide. Please do not interpret

---

[86] Msgr. William Smith, "The Place of a Tabernacle," *Homiletic and Pastoral Review* (December 1998).

[87] Duncan Stroik, "Environment and Art in Catholic Worship: A Critique," *Sacred Architecture* (Summer 1999).

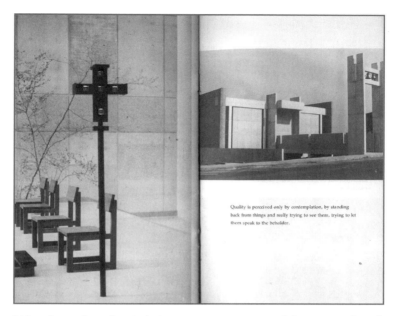

Quality is perceived only by contemplation, by standing back from things and really trying to see them, trying to let them speak to the beholder.

Aiding the modern church designers was a controversial document released by a subcommittee of bishops in 1978. Environment and Art in Catholic Worship *was described by Notre Dame architect Duncan Stroik as "a document of architectural reductionism that reflects a liturgical reductionism. It is fearful of symbols, complexity, history, art, and even architecture."*

this as an endorsement of the proposed redesign. But the design of worship space is not simply a matter of taste; all must come to terms with the directives from the Bishops."[88]

Just as the Second Vatican Council was first used to justify modern church architecture, EACW was later appealed to as the authoritative source. Yet whereas the council stated the opposite

[88] Duane L. C. M. Galles, J.C.D., "EACW: What Force Does It Have?" *Christifidelis* (September 8, 1993).

of what LDCs were doing in practice, EACW ratified what they had been doing all along. It was a manifesto made to order.

The practical recommendations of EACW were clearly based on architecture models and progressive liturgical theories popular in the 1960s. Edward Sövik, an Evangelical Lutheran architect from Minnesota, is representative of the leading theorists and practitioners of that time. His published articles began to appear in the late 1950s but most of them were published from 1960 to 1973. In 1973, Sövik published *Architecture for Worship,* a summary of his liturgical architecture ideas up to that time. Since then his treatise has been long used as a handbook by designers and renovators of Catholic and Protestant churches. In fact, Sövik himself has designed more than four hundred church-related projects in his career, both Catholic and Protestant.[89]

Sövik's book, along with *Church Architecture and Liturgical Reform* (1968), by Sövik's fellow architect Theodor Filthaut, effectively summarizes the archi-liturgical theories developed apart from but at the time of the Second Vatican Council. *Architecture for Worship* not only articulates the ideology behind Sövik's practical recommendations but it also forthrightly discloses his motivation and his desired results: to continue where the reformation Protestants left off four hundred years ago. An understanding of Sövik's 1973 ideology, which has been adopted by countless Catholic church design professionals, will help us understand the impetus driving church renovations and new churches designed and built since the '60s.

Sövik states his thesis thus:

The history of the church building through the Middle Ages is a record of a more explicit expression of a theology,

---

[89] Bette Hammel, "A New Architecture for Postwar America: Ed Sövik," *Architecture Minnesota* (November/December 1992).

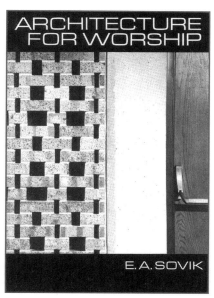

In 1973, Lutheran architect Edward Sövik published Architecture for Worship, *a summary of his liturgical architecture ideas up to that time. Since then, his treatise, reflected in EACW five years later, has been used as a handbook by designers and renovators of Catholic churches.*

E.A. SOVIK

a liturgy, and a piety that contradicted in important ways the essential message of Jesus. And when the Protestant and Catholic reformations of the sixteenth century came, the architectural forms that resulted were only partially corrective. The destruction of images and relics and the rearrangement of furniture in the existing buildings, and the sharp contrasts of form that appeared in some of the few new places of worship built in those times, did not effectively bring the minds of churchmen back into harmony with the minds of the early church.[90]

Sövik correctly states that architecture is more influential in the life of society than most people suppose. "The incompleteness

---

[90] E. A. Sövik, *Architecture for Worship*, 18.

of the Reformation in terms of architecture was no doubt the re-sult of the longevity of architecture," he explains. He laments that these medieval edifices aren't easily removed or changed, primar-ily because they were built as vertical and permanent structures to serve the Church until the end of time. To wit, even after the destructive iconoclasm of the Reformation, writes Sövik, "The 'houses of God' from medieval times continued to stand, contin-ued to assert themselves as 'houses of God' because of their strong ecclesial character, and continued to teach the people around them that there ought to be such a place as a 'house of God.' "[91]

He dismisses the enduring fact that churches built over a mil-lennia have "evolved" organically according to a desire to make visible Christ's presence in the world; he merely opines that nei-ther Jesus nor the Fathers of the Church wanted any such edifice, and we should work toward the elimination of such a "misguided medieval pattern." Sövik is further distressed that most of the churches built within the last four hundred years — both Catho-lic and Protestant — have continued to establish "holy places" more or less on what he mistakenly calls a medieval pattern.

To move beyond this pattern, Sövik argues for the return of the "non-church," or "house of the people," which he defines as a structure that shouldn't be a church but simply a place through which the people of the church can minister.

He writes, "Down through the centuries church buildings have not been consistently seen as exclusively places of worship. Church buildings have been multipurpose buildings, houses for people, used for a variety of public and secular activities that nourish the human and 'secular' life."[92] Sövik states this as the ideal for a litur-gical worship space, and he devotes his entire book to providing practical suggestions to accomplish this through architecture.

[91] Ibid., 19.
[92] Ibid.

He believes that in the United States, the Puritans and the Methodists once did this well: "The Puritans built meetinghouses, quite secular in form and detail, and used them for any public assembly. The early Methodists had their places of worship in any convenient barn or loft, and when they built, their architecture was consciously non-ecclesiastical."[93]

Like the early Methodist's prototype, Sövik's non-church should *not* be divided into a sanctuary and a nave. It shouldn't even be referred to using traditional terms of church architecture, lest, he worries, there be confusion. "It is a meeting place for people," he writes. "It will be so different a thing from the usual 'church' that any of these terms which carry the sense of special purpose liturgical centers is inappropriate."[94] Sövik proposes instead to use the word *centrum*. A centrum, he explains, "is a place for more than one purpose, and must be seen so, and so used. If it is not, if for one reason or another it is reserved for the Liturgy, it will sooner or later be thought of as the 'house of God'; and then it will be thought of as a holy place; and then other places will be seen as profane or secular."[95]

Sövik advocates a "throwaway" interior for his centrum. "For the space itself must be simple, allowing for many configurations of use. And the furnishings and symbolic devices will be portable, so they may be varied, replaced, augmented, or abandoned as the parishioners of future times desire."[96]

How, then, should one properly design the throwaway interior of a centrum that won't be mistaken by anyone to be a holy place or a house of God?

Sövik proposes the following in his book:

[93] Ibid., 21.
[94] Ibid., 68.
[95] Ibid., 70.
[96] Ibid., 71.

• Avoid the use of pews, and use only portable chairs;

• Set up a separate room to reserve the eucharistic species (if necessary);

• Avoid using any artwork that might be construed as strictly religious in content, e.g., paintings, murals, religious stat-ues, or icons;

• Avoid giving the impression of a sanctuary that is distinct from the nave by setting up a table in the midst of the con-gregation and arranging the chairs around that table;

• Avoid the use of crucifixes and Latin crosses in favor of portable Greek crosses ("plus signs") that would be used only in processions and during the Liturgy. Outside of liturgical times, no cross should be present in the worship space.

Many will recognize Sövik's recommendations as the same basic scheme that has been used repeatedly in the design or reno-vation of Catholic churches; it's the same practical advice offered in EACW.[97] Sövik didn't in fact intend his book only for his Protestant co-religionists, but marketed it as a handbook for Cath-olic and Protestant congregations: "[E]specially useful for church leaders, clergy, and building committees of Protestant and Roman Catholic churches, it offers practical, economical advice on both the remodeling of existing structures and the construction of new

---

[97] EACW is generally accepted as primarily the work of one man: Fr. Robert Hovda. The late Fr. Hovda wrote the fore-word to the 1968 book *Church Architecture and Liturgical Reform,* written by one of Sövik's architecture associates, Theodor Filthaut. EACW was never approved by the body of U.S. bishops and was eventually replaced by the U.S. bishops' pastoral on church art and architecture, *Built of Living Stones,* approved in 2000.

*Modern church designers recommend that neither
a crucifix nor a Latin cross be used. Following Sövik's practical
principles from the 1970s, they prefer the use of the Greek cross,
which is shaped like a plus sign. Sövik wrote that this form is
obscure enough not to be identified with the sacrificial Cross of Jesus.*

ones."[98] In other words, here was a Protestant architect with a decidedly Protestant viewpoint advocating the reform of Catholic church architecture to conform with his Protestant theology and ecclesiology.

The theory on which Sövik's proposal is predicated is both interesting and revealing. He begins by making some observations on what he considers to be "good liturgical space": It should be one space, he suggests; its horizontal proportions should not be too elongated so as not to give the impression of a traditional rectangular church arrangement, which he sees as problematic. "The

[98] Sövik, *Architecture for Worship*, back cover.

design tradition we have inherited from the Renaissance," he writes, "has led us to assume that every large room should be organized symmetrically, and we tend to look for some dominating feature about which the room comes to focus. If we declare that *people* are really the focus of what happens in the Liturgy, then any very strong architectural focus can subvert our intentions."[99] Accordingly Sövik argues against the tabernacle, the crucifix, and the altar, each of which tends to become a focal point in what he calls "liturgical space."

Instead of using Renaissance or medieval church plans as precedents for the design of his non-church centrum, Sövik proposes that designers look for prototypes in the vernacular architecture of the Japanese tea house[100] and in the dining room/living room combos that became popular in post-World War II houses. His practical recommendations are consistent with these prototypes, which, according to Sövik, provide "a place for people to gather and share their lives with one another."

[99] Ibid., 76.

[100] "The [Japanese] tea house is usually related to a garden, which provides a pathway to it, and one never loses his relationship to the exterior world. Even when the paper windows are closed and the door is shut so that one cannot see the world outside, the forthright use of building materials and structural systems keeps one aware that this is an earthly place. It is conventional, for instance, that a tea house never has a ceiling; the structure supporting the bark or thatch roof is exposed. And the tan plaster is not painted. It is a humbly built shelter without the slightest attempt at grandeur or impressiveness, but its design is very sensitive and the craftsmanship extremely careful. It is in no sense a monument and does not have an autonomous existence like a shrine. It is a building built for use, and has an apparent sense of emptiness when it is unoccupied": Edward A. Sövik, "Images of the Church," *Worship* (March 1967).

*Sövik's ideology boils down to a secularization of
the sacred in church architecture. Accordingly, he advocated
"non-churches" that are "quite secular in form and detail."*

Sövik's recommendations were echoed by EACW five years later.

On the issue of pews or chairs, Sövik writes, "Nothing gives the conventional church building its ecclesiastical character more than do pews, and nothing inhibits flexibility more than pews. Chairs have the advantages of flexibility."[101] Discard the pews, then, he recommends, and replace them with portable stackable chairs that you might find in a school, restaurant, or conference hall. Again, Sövik doesn't want anyone to mistake his centrum for a church.

[101] Sövik, *Architecture for Worship*, 77.

161

EACW in a similar fashion recommends, "When multi-function use of the space is indicated by the needs of either the faith community or of the surrounding city, town, or rural area which the faith community services, a certain flexibility or movability should be considered even for the essential furnishings."[102] Since pews offer neither flexibility nor movability, the church renovator argues that portable stackable chairs are ideal. Even when multifunction use of the space isn't indicated, the non-church designer will still often advocate the chair over the pew; it's the fashion of the day.

On the elimination of the sanctuary, Sövik writes, "It should be recognized that the intent of a dais or platform is not to accent a sanctuary as separate from the congregation space. It is simply to provide enough elevation so that certain liturgical functions which need visibility can get it."[103] The non-church should be all sanctuary or all nave.

EACW addresses the topic in a more nuanced manner, yet arrives at the same result: "Special attention must be given to the *unity of the entire liturgical space*. Before considering the distinction of roles within the Liturgy, the space should communicate integrity (a sense of oneness, of wholeness) and a sense of being the gathering place of the initiated community."[104]

Writing about the "eucharistic table," Sövik states, "The eucharistic table is usually called an altar, but ought to be distinguished from the sacrificial altars of other religions. Its genus is the dining room table. It is the table at which the ritual meal is served,

[102] EACW, no. 65.
[103] Sövik, *Architecture for Worship*, 81.
[104] EACW, no. 53.

and its symbolic value is like that of the dining table in the home. The eucharistic table ought to be located where it can be sensed as belonging to the whole gathered community."[105]

In its section on the altar, EACW recommends that the "holy *table*" be designed for the "action of the community." It should therefore "not be elongated, but square or slightly rectangular . . . [and] central in any eucharistic celebration."[106] LDCs are fond of interpreting this section of EACW as a ringing endorsement of throwing the altar "into the midst of the people." The important sacrificial aspect of the Mass is dismissed.

Sövik also argues for the elimination of kneeling to receive Communion because, he claims, "a celebration ought to be joyful, but kneeling is not the posture of joy; in a communion one ought to be particularly conscious of the community; . . . but kneeling is not a posture in which we can properly commune."[107]

EACW offers no advice on accommodating the traditional posture of kneeling during the Liturgy; it only exhorts designers to strive for "a seating pattern and furniture that do not constrict people, but encourage them to move about when it is appropriate."[108] Although one wonders how often it's "appropriate" to move about during the Mass, the church renovator interprets that exhortation as justification for seating without kneelers, since kneelers tend to "constrict" people.[109]

---

[105] Sövik, *Architecture for Worship*, 83.

[106] EACW, no. 72.

[107] Sövik, *Architecture for Worship*, 87.

[108] EACW, no. 68.

[109] Prominent church renovator Fr. Richard Vosko is fond of saying, "When we get to the pearly gates, God isn't going to ask

On the issue of visual projections, Sövik argues that in new buildings and remodeled churches, technology for visual projection and moving pictures must be accommodated. "If a church can provide a good place for cinema, it has an additional way of serving a community and making a building more useful."[110]

> Five years later, EACW makes the same recommendation in paragraph 104: "It is safe to say that a new church building or renovation project should make provision for screens and/or walls which will make the projection of films, slides, and filmstrips visible to the entire assembly."

Sövik also demands that never are recognizable crucifixes to be used: "The iconoclastic reformers removed the corpus and left the Protestants with a symbol which is the image of an instrument of torture. We have become used to this curiosity so that we most often forget what it is, or suppose the absence of a corpus is an adequate symbol for resurrection. Would an electric chair symbolize resurrection? Or would we accept the electric chair as a proper symbol of the Christian Faith if Jesus had been executed in this century?"[111] Thus, Sövik recommends that neither the crucifix nor the traditional Latin cross be used. He argues for use of the so-called Greek cross, which appears in the shape of a plus sign. He believes that this form is obscure enough not to be identified with the sacrificial cross, the "instrument of torture." Sövik, also opposed to large crosses, argues for a single, "small" processional cross ("one doesn't need to suppose that there must be a gigantic symbol somewhere, as if making a cross big demonstrates superior

us whether we had kneelers, but God will ask us if we fed the hungry": Ethel M. Gintoff, "Cathedral renovation: Enhance liturgy, don't destroy, says design consultant," *Catholic Herald* (June 24, 1999): 1.

[110] Sövik, *Architecture for Worship*, 91.

[111] Ibid., 109.

piety," he writes), one that is "among the people" during the Liturgy and whisked away at its completion.

So, too, EACW recommends, instead of a large fixed cross or crucifix, "a processional cross with a floor standard, in contrast to one that is permanently hung or affixed to a wall."[112] And although the Greek cross isn't specifically called for by EACW, the church renovator consistently advocates the use of the "plus-sign-shaped cross."

Sövik concludes his treatise by illustrating his ideal of the throwaway non-church centrum. He cites the work of St. Katherine's parish in Baltimore, Maryland (remember, this is back in 1973):

Here Fr. Joseph Connolly, a priest whose sense of liturgy and human concern belong together, is leading the parish to immerse themselves in providing for the welfare of the people in the area. He now calls his church building a 'community service center.' The nave has been cleared of pews and other hindrances. It has become the meeting place for any kind of assembly that needs a place, and movable screens can separate different kinds of activities that occur simultaneously. Children swarm. Rock music, dances, clinics, educational enterprises, eating and drinking, even a homosexual group have been given shelter. For if Jesus didn't reject the company of publicans and prostitutes, why should the church be less hospitable?[113]

Catholic LDCs have been viscerally affected by Sövik and his ideological allies such as Filthaut, J. G. Davies (author of *The Secular Use of Church Buildings*, 1968), and Frederic Dubyst (author of

[112] EACW, no. 88.
[113] Sövik, *Architecture for Worship*, 118-119.

Modern Architecture and Christian Celebration) for the past four decades at least. Sövik has enjoyed guru status among the Catholic design consultants, his architectural work is held up as exemplary, and he's regarded by many LDCs as a mentor. Indeed, his archiliturgical ideology of secularizing the sacred was *en vogue* among liturgists during the mid-1970s as it still is at the turn of the century. Sövik and kindred spirits were caught up with the liturgical experimentation of the late 1960s and early '70s. Their penultimate goal, clearly enunciated in their written works, was the elimination of the sacred from church architecture; their ultimate goal, the elimination of the church building in favor of a secular meeting house to be used on occasion for religious purposes.

EACW doesn't discuss its goals. Nevertheless, in the opinion of Notre Dame architect Duncan Stroik, "it seems that the BCL produced a document worthy of the 'non church' promoted by Protestant architect Sövik."[114] Indeed, the practical recommendations offered by Sövik in 1973 to create his ideal throwaway, non-church centrum are the same practical recommendations offered by the Bishops' Committee on Liturgy in their controversial 1978 document.

⌒

*Architects have deliberately
secularized our Catholic churches*

The ultimate purpose of effecting a paradigm shift in Catholic church architecture is radically to remake Catholicism by striking at the outward manifestations of the Catholic Faith. The old paradigm of nearly fifteen hundred years that Sövik rejects is one of "familiarity" and "mystery," a holy building set in a place that gave the community a sense of continuity and security. Fr. Richard

[114] Duncan Stroik, "Environment and Art in Catholic Worship: A Critique."

Vosko, a Catholic priest and probably the most renowned LDC, elaborates on this idea:

> The architectural style and furnishings in the [American] neighborhood churches were similar in many ways to those in European homelands. The quiet ambience, the ubiquitous smell of incense, the flicker of candles dancing in the darkness, the almost eerie presence of innumerable images, laser-like beams streaming through stained-glass windows, immense high altars, and the surreptitious presentation of the Mass contributed to the familiar and mysterious milieu. My boyhood church was the church of immigrants clinging to the past for continuity and identity. It sustained what people believed to be expressions of mystery. It was where God dwelled.[115]

In contrast, the new paradigm reflects the ideology and practical recommendations of Sövik's parish centrum. Fr. Vosko, who at the time of this writing is employed by seven U.S. cathedrals[116] as an LDC, echoes Sövik when he describes his ideal "church of tomorrow" as one that's primarily secular: "similar to the other familiar public spaces, buildings that are well designed and constructed to accommodate large numbers of people in comfortable and pleasant ways."[117]

He writes hopefully that the church of tomorrow:[118]

---

[115] Fr. Richard S. Vosko, "The future space of worship spaces: in between no more and not yet," *The Catholic World* (March-April 1994).

[116] In mid-2001, Fr. Vosko was contracted by cathedrals in Los Angeles, California; Milwaukee, Wisconsin; Superior, Wisconsin; San Antonio, Texas; St. Petersburg, Florida; Colorado Springs, Colorado; and Rochester, New York.

[117] Vosko, "The future space of worship spaces."

[118] Ibid.

• will "tell the 'faith stories' of this age";

• will "be mysterious not because of any architectural or artistic sleight of hand but because of the respectful and gracious way people conduct themselves";

• will "become, once again, a house for the church" (rather than a "house of God");

• will use "sophisticated building materials and technologies, not the natural and more expensive materials used in the churches of the past";

• will "focus on the assembly gathered about the font and table";

• will "stimulate the senses through the incorporation of mobile art, holography, and computerized projections";

• will incorporate natural scents to "trigger the full sensual capacity of the community causing interactive, conscious, and subliminal participation in the celebration of word and sacrament";

• will more fully integrate music, singing, drama, and body movement into the worship action;

• will include "other sectors" devoted to bible study, prayer sessions, counseling, and support groups;

• will have a database of biographies so that the community may be able "to interact with holographic images of religious folk heroes";

• will feature sculptures, weavings, and paintings of "saintly personalities" in its "inner and outer gardens and pathways";

• will house the "eucharistic bread" in "its own chapel sector."

Fr. Richard Vosko, probably the most well known of Catholic liturgical design consultants, echoed Sövik's ideals when he described his ideal "church of tomorrow" as one that is primarily secular: "similar to other familiar public spaces." (Yes, this is such a church.)

Fr. Vosko's most prominent project, the new Our Lady of the Angels Cathedral in Los Angeles, reflects this new paradigm in a grand way and violates the natural laws of church architecture. First, the new cathedral bears no resemblance in form or substance to cathedral churches of past centuries. (It has been described by critics in L.A. as a "yellow armadillo."[119]) Christian iconography on the façades is minimal, and the symbolism that is used is said to be more "inclusive" and "universally appealing" than specifically Catholic. One Archdiocese of Los Angeles official explained that

[119] Jill Stewart, "Yellow Armadillo," *New Times L.A.* (July 28, 2001).

"you don't need St. Peter and St. Paul over the entrance." Rather, he admitted, the new Our Lady of the Angels cathedral "avoids as-signing meaning," although in the same breath he begrudgingly conceded that the L.A. cathedral "obviously will have a certain amount of rhetoric brought into it because it has a certain use."[120]

Defending his transgression of the natural law of permanence, Fr. Vosko explained that the church doesn't even pretend to be transcendent of time or culture. "This cathedral," he remarked to the press, "is of its own time, of its own liturgy, of its own people."[121] Fr. Vosko added that he wasn't interested in establishing a sacred place like the European cathedrals of past centuries. Rather, he explained, it isn't even possible to accomplish such a thing. All one can do is to create an "architectural form that would house the ritual forms of a particular religion, whether it's Jewish, Catholic, Muslim, or whatnot."[122] With this dim view, the faceless façade is appropriate for the modern non-church centrum. It's an accurate prelude to the worship space within, one that is no less inspiring or sacred than its antecedent.

❧

Modern church designs violate the natural laws of church architecture

It's quite obvious that the "non-church," the new paradigm in church architecture, doesn't reflect a desire to make Christ visibly present in a particular locale or to manifest the Catholic Faith through built form. Few churches of this new paradigm truly serve as epicenters or souls of their communities, to say the least. No one will ever write a "biography" of the renovated St. John's

[120] Reed Johnson, "A Modern Sense of the Sacred," *Los Angeles Times* (May 22, 2001).
[121] Vosko, "The future space of worship spaces."
[122] Ibid.

Cathedral in Milwaukee. No one will write a novel about St. Mary's Cathedral in Gaylord, Michigan, about Corpus Christi Church in Toledo, or about the Millennium Church in Rome, designed by Richard Meier. Few will make pilgrimages to cathedrals in Las Vegas, Oakland, or Los Angeles. These are buildings that leave doubts in the mind of the pilgrim about whether they're Catholic churches; they're places, judging from all appearances, where you must search out the tabernacle as if it were the lost Ark of the Covenant.

These non-churches — and thousands like them built since 1960 — are buildings that don't speak of God, don't turn man's mind, heart, and soul to things eternal. They're merely "skins for liturgical action," lifeless, banal, and uninspiring, often ugly. What pilgrim could gaze on St. John's Abbey in Collegeville, Minnesota, and conclude that it's a beautiful edifice raised to the greater glory of God? What passerby could look at Oakland's cathedral and think of anything but a giant clam?

Inasmuch as the new paradigm worship spaces adhere to Sövik's non-church formula, they can't rightly be regarded as houses of God — Sövik will be happy — but simply as spaces in which people meet from time to time to participate in the Mass, which the building's architecture has reduced to a nearly meaningless ritual. The sacrificial aspects of the Holy Sacrifice are hidden from the senses — no crucifix, no prominent altar, no religious imagery. The architectural language used to design the non-church dismisses the great works of the past to embrace the liturgical fashion of the day, one that can and will be discarded in years to come to make way for newer trends, fads, and fashions. The pilgrim will find no colonnades, arched windows, impressive domes, or wooden pews.

Because the non-church lacks verticality, the pilgrim isn't likely to be inspired to the other worldly. Without permanence, the new paradigm church is ephemeral — here today, gone tomorrow.

Devoid of any iconography that speaks of God and eternity, the non-church fails to inspire, to evangelize, to teach, or to attract. In fact, it may do the opposite. The new paradigm edifice may actually repel people, may drive them further from the truth of the Faith, and may convey a message that says Christ and His Church really aren't that important.

At best, the new paradigm church is mere human folly, an expensive experiment, a failed architecture. It can't transcend time and culture. It's merely a product of its own time, a consumer item that will be quickly expended and will offer little or nothing to future generations. In the new paradigm, meaning isn't conveyed through built form or religious art; meaning is the enemy. Verticality, permanence, and iconography give way to the horizontal, ephemeral, and iconoclastic. Goodness, beauty, and truth become evil, ugliness, and deceit.

Modern church designs threaten the faith of Catholics

The built environment has always shaped human behavior. In fact, this is why architects such as Edward Sövik and liturgical consultants such as Fr. Richard Vosko are so dedicated to promoting their designs. They know well that the built environment influences how Catholics worship. They also know that how Catholics worship affects what they believe, because worship is really a reflection of belief (*lex orandi, lex credendi*). It's difficult, if not impossible to separate theology and ecclesiology from the environment for worship, whether it's a traditional church or a modern non-church centrum. If a Catholic church building doesn't reflect Catholic theology and ecclesiology, it's hard for the pilgrim to accept that building as a proper place for Catholic worship, whether public liturgy or private devotions. If he does accept it as a proper place of worship, he risks accepting a faith that's foreign to Catholicism.

Why modern architects secularized our churches

The modern non-church, to be sure, doesn't reflect Catholic theology or ecclesiology. Rather, it reflects the desires, hopes, aspirations, and philosophies of architects like Sövik, who by his own admission doesn't accept the Catholic creed, the Catholic form of worship, or Catholic ecclesiology. For instance, he doesn't believe in the Catholic doctrine of the Real Presence. His modern church worship spaces reflect his disavowal of this important Catholic belief. Nor does he accept that the Catholic Mass is a holy sacrifice, a re-presentation of Christ's Sacrifice on Calvary. This disavowal of the sacrifice is also reflected in the design of his modern churches as well as articulated in his influential writings, which have affected Catholic liturgists and designers for four decades.

In fact, the modern non-church promoted by Sövik is a repudiation of Catholic theology, ecclesiology, worship, belief, and tradition. Contrary to what we learn in the *Catechism of the Catholic Church*, the non-church is predicated on the idea that the universal Church should not establish "holy places." It denies the vertical, because the non-church is built, not to the greater glory of God, but for a gathering of the people. It can't admit the possibility of a church that's both functional for people and gives glory to God through its beauty and majesty. It denies permanency by breaking with historical models and through its emphasis on the "flexibility doctrine," which purports that a worship space must not be created specifically for liturgical and devotional purposes with fixed furnishings. It denies that a sacred place can teach, evangelize, catechize, and inspire. In a word, it's iconoclastic.

Few will contest that many modern non-churches are aesthetically unsettling. Nonetheless, the notion of "ugly" as used in the title of this book (*Ugly as Sin*) refers not just to that which is aesthetically offensive, but also to that which is theologically inappropriate: the modern non-church engenders responses in worshipers that are wrong, leading them away from the goodness, beauty, and truth of the Faith to a false notion of God and of themselves in the face of God.

Because the modern non-church implies a false theology, it's theologically ugly — literally, ugly as sin.

Chapter Five

⌒

How we can make our churches Catholic again
(or, what the Vatican wants you to do
to help restore the Faith in our day)

With hindsight, many are waking up to the fact that the experimental church architecture designed and built in the latter half of the twentieth century has miserably failed the Catholic people. The innovative forms used by church architects in the '60s and '70s look not only outdated at the dawn of the new century; they look ugly. The non-churches of the '80s and '90s that can pass for libraries, post offices, or nursing homes are so uninspiring and banal that they fail to attract, to evangelize, or to raise the hearts and minds of man to God. They fail to acknowledge that Christ was made flesh and dwelt among us. They fail to serve the Catholic community, and they fail to make Christ's presence known in any particular place. Similarly, the insensitive renovation of traditional churches that stripped these sacred edifices of their Catholic trappings, not only denuded a physical place, but also altered the worship and beliefs of the people.

Fortunately, however, the growing realization and acknowledgment of this failure — on the part of laity, priests, bishops, and architects alike — is the first step that will lead to the renewal of our sacred places. Designer Francis X. Gibbons, for instance, now speaks of his 1968 renovation of St. Mary, Star of the Sea Church in Baltimore as a "raping" of that church.[123] Helen Marikle Passano, the primary patron for the restoration of the 1869 chapel at Notre Dame College in Baltimore, remembers loving the "modernization" of the chapel when she was a student there. "We thought we were moving forward with a contemporary space. But guess what? We're moving back," she told the *Baltimore Sun* in early 2001. "It's time to bring [the chapel] back to its original glory." To this end, she donated $1.5 million to peel away the 1960s alterations, "including a flat ceiling and metal ducts that obscured the vaulted spaces above, wood paneling that covered plaster walls, and carpeting that smothered the handsome pine floor."[124] Even the Vatican finally addressed the renovation problem in 2001, when Cardinal Jorge Medina Estevez, prefect for the Congregation for Divine Worship, informed Archbishop Rembert Weakland of Milwaukee that his proposed cathedral renovation didn't conform to Church norms or liturgical law and was doing a disservice to Milwaukee Catholics.[125]

This realization period should lead to four distinct ways to improve the architecture of Catholic churches, transforming these edifices from meeting spaces into sacred places:

• *Restore traditional Catholic churches*. That is, architects and pastors must work together to return to their former glory the older, traditionally oriented buildings that were renovated over the past three or four decades.

---

[123] " 'I've often said after I did that job,' said Francis X. Gibbons, the man who designed the renovation, 'that I raped St. Mary, Star of the Sea' ": John Rivers, "Churches try to retrieve grand trappings of past," *Baltimore Sun* (May 21, 2001).

[124] Edward Gunts, "Happy undoing of a modernist makeover," *Baltimore Sun* (March 4, 2001).

[125] Letter from Cardinal Jorge Medina Estevez to Archbishop Rembert Weakland, July 2, 2001.

In 2001, Notre Dame College in Baltimore embarked on a project (above) to restore its chapel to its original beauty. The project will peel away the 1960s alterations (below left) to the 1869 church (below right).

• *Salvage and renovate the modernist churches* built in the latter half of the twentieth century by reorienting them and endowing them with verticality, iconography, and permanency. Many of the buildings erected during the '60s and '70s, although irregular in form, can be transformed into beautiful transcendent places within.

• *Transform ugly, modernist churches into parish halls or school buildings, and build replacement churches* that will serve as genuine sacred places, designed in continuity with the Church's tradition and adhering to the natural laws of church architecture.

• *Build beautiful churches anew when parishes are established.*

⌒

We must restore churches that were
marred by fashionable renovations

At the dawn of the twenty-first century, a new trend is emerging: some of the churches that were drastically altered decades ago are now being restored to their former beauty.

For example, when Bishop Bernard J. Flanagan returned to Worcester, Massachusetts, after the Second Vatican Council, one of the first ways he sought to implement the "spirit of Vatican II" was by remodeling his cathedral church. No doubt influenced by the spirit of change that swept through Western society during the tumultuous '60s, he oversaw the removal of the sacred furnishings that had come to be universally identified with the Catholic sanctuary. In place of the reredos and high altar, a concrete block wall was erected, and a simple freestanding wooden altar table was introduced. The walls were whitewashed, mustard-yellow carpeting was installed, the communion rail was removed, and a new, unadorned tabernacle that could be mistaken for a mailbox was set on a pillar in a side alcove.

At the dawn of the twenty-first century, a new trend is emerging: some of the churches that were drastically altered decades ago are now being restored to their former beauty. St. Mary's Church in downtown Rockford, Illinois, was restored by the Institute of Christ the King Sovereign Priest.

Ugly as Sin

Three decades later, shortly after Daniel P. Reilly was made Bishop of Worcester in 1994, he announced an interior restoration project that would restore the cathedral's sanctuary. The concrete block wall was removed, and an ornate hand-carved wood reredos and a noble cathedra were erected in its place. Statues of Sts. Peter and Paul were moved back into the sanctuary. The tabernacle was given proper prominence and ornamentation, and a shrine to Our Lady of Guadalupe was fashioned from the leftover wood of the sanctuary project. The mustard-yellow carpeting was removed, and the walls and ceiling of the church's interior were repainted to match the original multicolor scheme. The church's interior, thanks to Bishop Reilly and architect Rolf Rohn, now no longer looks dated from 1968. The restoration carried out in 1996 was in keeping with the building's original design.

Numerous churches, from small rural parishes to urban cathedrals, have been undergoing similar restorations. St. Patrick's Church in Forest City, Missouri, for instance, underwent a restoration to bring it more in line with its original look. Following Vatican II, this church, built in 1906, was "modernized" by way of a drop ceiling and wood-paneled walls. The Stations of the Cross, the old altar, several statues, and other sacred furnishings were removed from the church. In 1999, however, the new pastor, Father Joseph Hughes, initiated a restoration. Fortunately, some parishioners had saved items that were removed from the church during the previous renovation thirty years before. A sanctuary lamp, the old tabernacle, and candlesticks were refurbished and incorporated into the new design. Just as at St. Paul's Cathedral in Worcester, a new reredos is the highlight of the sanctuary renovation at St. Patrick's. Patterned after the church's old altar, it sits behind the new altar and holds the altar crucifix and statuary.

These examples provide models for what can be done to reorient a renovated church. The first step must always be to restore the hierarchical form. The sanctuary must be made distinct again

In 1996, architect Rolf Rohn restored the Cathedral of St. Paul in Worcester, Massachusetts, returning the church's interior to much of its original splendor. (Top: before the 1968 renovation; bottom left: after the 1968 renovation; bottom right: after the 1996 renovation.)

from the nave, where the congregation sits. In many cases, this will mean that altars that have been moved into the midst of the congregation must be returned to a proper sanctuary. The altar platform — usually consisting of one or two steps — that sits out in the nave with chairs gathered around isn't a sufficiently defined sanctuary by any means. Most, if not all, traditional churches are designed in the basilican cruciform plan. That means that there already exists a proper location for the sanctuary: at the elevated "head" of the building. The nave serves as the body.

In other renovated churches, the sanctuary has been moved to one of the nave's side walls and the entire building reoriented so that when you enter the church building, there's no natural progression down an aisle toward the altar of sacrifice. This type of renovation is really just a disorientation. Here, the sanctuary needs to be restored to its proper position at the head of the building and the nave reoriented to lead once again toward the restored altar.

The sanctuary should also be redefined, that is, if the raised platform of the sanctuary has been removed, it must be restored. If the communion railing has been eliminated, the restoration of such a device will provide a distinct boundary for the sanctuary, and it will also be functional if Communion is distributed to communicants kneeling at the restored railing. The design of a restored railing should match the architecture of the church and the altar especially.

But in many cases, the altar in renovated churches is itself inadequate. The poorly designed table altars that replaced high altars of past centuries can be deficient in several respects. First, they're often crafted of wood alone. To focus again on its sacrificial nature, the altar ought to include an altar stone, a plain horizontal slab on which the priest places the Holy Sacrifice of the Mass. The restored altar should also be a permanent fixture, built of durable materials. A simple table that could be used for a thanksgiving dinner in our homes is insufficient.

There's no reason why dignified altars can't be designed and built anew, complemented by either a beautiful reredos or baldacchino. The altar and baldacchino of the Warwick House Chapel in Pittsburgh were designed by Henry Hardinge Menzies in 1992.

In some renovated churches, the high altar fortunately still remains, although it has often served only to hold flowers or candlesticks since a freestanding altar was introduced after Vatican II. In these fortunate churches, the most obvious solution is to eliminate the inadequate freestanding altar and revert to using the high altar, which is often already the natural focal point of the church, accented by either a reredos or baldacchino.

In many other churches, however, the high altar and reredos or baldacchino have been summarily removed. Although this is a most unfortunate situation, for those parishes that are committed to restoration it can be an opportunity to design and build something even more worthy and beautiful than the original. Such is the case with St. Paul's Cathedral in Worcester, already mentioned. It's also the case with several traditional churches that were restored in the diocese of Victoria, Texas. This diocese is noted for its preservation of the famous "painted churches" in the Schulenburg area. Some of these churches had lost many of their sanctuary furnishings shortly after the Second Vatican Council. A generation later, however, nine parishes in the Victoria diocese tried to recapture what they had lost. The ornate high altar and reredos at St. Joseph's Church in Moulton, Texas, for instance, was completely reconstructed from scratch by local carpenters in 1994.

There really is no reason why dignified altars can't be made anew, complemented either by a beautiful reredos or baldacchino, depending on the style and design of the church. These elements will not only bring the focus back to the altar, but they will also ennoble it.

⁓

We must return the tabernacle to its place behind the altar
Another important — perhaps the most important — aspect of a sanctuary restoration is moving the tabernacle back to its original position in the center of the sanctuary, behind the altar. In

1997 Fr. Richard Simon of St. Thomas of Canterbury Church in Chicago blazed a trail in this regard. He announced to his parish that he planned to make such a liturgical move because he felt that the experiment of removing the tabernacle from the sanctuary had failed. In his June 24, 1997 letter to his parishioners, he wrote:

> I believe that much of the liturgical experimentation that began thirty years ago has failed. We are not holier, nor more Christ-centered now than we were then. In fact, we are facing a generation of young people who are largely lost to the Church because we have not given them the precious gift that is at the heart of Catholicism, that is, the Real Presence of Jesus. Mass has become simply a drama, a vehicle for whatever agenda is currently popular. The church building is no longer a place of encounter with the Lord but a sort of a social center, not a place of prayer, rather a place of chatter.
>
> In many churches, including our own, the tabernacle was moved from the center of the church to add emphasis to Mass and the presence of the Lord in the reception of Holy Communion. That experiment, however, has failed. We have lost the sense of the sacred that formerly was the hallmark of Catholic worship. The behavior of many in the church is outrageous. When Mass is over it is impossible to spend time in prayer. The noise level reaches the pitch that one would expect at a sporting event. The kiss of peace seems like New Year's Eve. Christ is forgotten on the altar. You may counter that He is present in the gathering of the Church, and though this is true, it should not detract from the Lord present on the altar. If the Lord is truly recognized in the congregation, it should serve to enhance the sacredness of the moment. This is simply not happening. . . .

Ugly as Sin

Therefore, I have decided to restore the tabernacle to its former place in the middle of the sanctuary and to begin a campaign of re-education as to the sacredness of worship and the meaning of the Real Presence. This means that I will nag and nag until a sense of the sacred is restored. I will be reminding you that a respectful quiet will have to be maintained in church. Food and toys and socializing are welcome elsewhere, but the church is the place of an encounter with the Living God. It will not be a popular policy, but this is unimportant.

I can hear one objection already. Where will the priest sit? I will sit where the priest has traditionally sat, over on the side of the sanctuary. Here as in many churches the "presider's" chair was placed where the tabernacle had been. I am sick of sitting on the throne that should belong to my Lord. The dethronement of the Blessed Sacrament has resulted in the enthronement of the clergy, and I for one am sick of it. The Mass has become priest-centered. The celebrant is everything. I am a sinner saved by grace as you are and not the center of the Eucharist. Let me resume my rightful place before the Lord rather than instead of the Lord. I am ordained to the priesthood of Christ in the order of presbyter, and as such I do have a special and humbling role. I am elder brother in the Lord and with you I seek to follow Him and to worship. Please, please let me return Christ to the center of our life together where He belongs.

Once Fr. Simon returned the tabernacle to its former location at the center of the sanctuary behind the altar, he was surprised, he said, at the response. It was overwhelmingly positive and effective. A sense of reverence was indeed restored at Mass in his church. On September 16, 1997, he reported the results of the move:

You cannot imagine the response I got to the letter I addressed to my parishioners on June 24. I have received so many calls and letters that I am reduced to saying thank you in a form letter. Still, I simply have to write to say thank you for your support and prayers. So many people thought I was brave to do what I did. Brave? I simply read the *Catechism* and moved a few pieces of furniture. The response has been overwhelmingly positive. In the parish, some people even wept for joy when they saw the change. I am still kicking myself and asking why I didn't do this years ago. The response has been so supportive. Many wrote and expressed their sense of loneliness in the battle for Catholic orthodoxy. Well, you are not alone, neither among the laity nor the clergy.

Perhaps you have heard the definition of a neo-conservative. He is a liberal who has been mugged by reality. That certainly describes me. I was in college in the late Sixties and went the whole route: beard, sandals, protest, leafleting for feminism, and all the rest. . . . [I]f a parish like this and a person like me can be turned from foolish liturgical experimentation, it can happen anywhere to anyone. Don't give up! For instance, if they have taken the kneelers out of your church, go to the front and kneel on the hard floor. You'll be amazed how many will join you. That's what's happened here.

Inspired by this well-publicized move by Fr. Simon, many pastors have restored the tabernacle to prominence in their churches. This, as he attests, was simply "moving furniture," but it restored the kind of prayerful reverence in his church that he and many others desired. With the tabernacle directly behind the altar on the building's main axis, the two elements work together as one: the tabernacle was returned to an extension of the altar, which is the focal point of the church, just as the Blessed Sacrament is an extension of the Holy Sacrifice of the Mass. Since the reserved Sacrament is an extension of the Mass, it logically follows that, architecturally speaking, the tabernacle ought to be situated in direct relationship to the altar, whether on the altar or behind it. This arrangement has ramifications far beyond interior design. Ultimately, it is a matter of devotion and worship.

According to Pope John Paul II, proper devotion to the Blessed Sacrament will inevitably lead to a fuller participation in the eucharistic celebration. In his letter on the 750th anniversary of the Feast of Corpus Christi, he wrote, "Outside the eucharistic celebration, the Church is careful to venerate the Blessed Sacrament, which must be reserved . . . as the spiritual center of the religious and parish community. Contemplation prolongs Communion and enables one to meet Christ, true God and true man, in a lasting way. . . . Prayer of adoration in the presence of the Blessed Sacrament unites the faithful with the paschal mystery; it enables them to share in Christ's sacrifice, of which the Eucharist is the permanent sacrament."[126]

Tied in to this theology of the Eucharist is the crucifix, the figural representation of Christ's Sacrifice on Calvary, that which is re-presented in an unbloody manner by the hands of the ordained priest at the altar. As mentioned before, the crucifix — the corpus of Christ on the Cross — was removed from many churches during renovations and replaced by either symbolic processional crosses or other figures, such as the risen Christ or paintings of wheat, sun, and birds. As beneficial as these new symbols may be to some, the restoration of the crucifix is integral to a proper restoration of the sanctuary. It is the crucifix that directly symbolizes the whole meaning of the Mass.

---

[126] John Paul II, "Letter on the 750th Anniversary of the Feast of Corpus Christi," no. 3.

Another important — perhaps the most important — aspect
of sanctuary restoration is moving the tabernacle to the
center of the sanctuary, behind the altar. The restoration of the
sanctuary at St. Aloysius Church in New Canaan, Connecticut,
included positioning the tabernacle behind the altar as the centerpiece
of the glass reredos. The restoration of the crucifix, which symbolizes
the meaning of the Mass, is also integral to a proper sanctuary restoration.

Ugly as Sin

⌒

We must restore the sacred art
that was stripped from our churches

Another element especially significant to the restoration of the sanctuary is the restoration of sacred art. Many unfortunate churches were whitewashed thirty years ago in an iconoclastic attempt to remove so-called distractions from the house of God en route to reducing the church to a non-church. Others had their statues summarily removed for the same reason. Fortunately, these misguided purges have begun to wane, yet plenty of churches have been left barren and stripped because some pastor, liturgist, or designer was a slave to fashion, bad taste, or wrongheaded theology. This is what church designer Francis X. Gibbons called "rape."

But not all is lost. With the newest methods of art preservation and restoration, murals and frescoes can be recovered, whitewashed statues can be returned to their original colors, and deteriorated works of sacred art can be restored. Such advances in the art of preservation ought to give hope to many a pastor who desires to bring the sacred back into his church building.

Furthermore, there are, contrary to public understanding, talented artists who can be commissioned to execute beautiful new murals or mosaics in churches that are unable to recover their artistic patrimony.

With regard to statues, icons, and other pieces of "movable" art, there exists a treasury of old sacred art available at architectural antique shops around the United States and beyond. A few calls can put a pastor or restorationist in touch with groups that have salvaged these often priceless works of art from Catholic parishes that have been closed and their churches razed.

The same goes for architectural furnishings such as old wooden confessionals, sacred vessels, crucifixes, Stations of the Cross, pews, and communion rails. Some of the more well-known Internet auction web sites, for instance, offer a steady supply of these beautiful works of art. Unfortunately, these items more often wind up being used for secular purposes rather than in new or restored churches. We've all heard of confessionals being used as telephone booths in restaurants or ornate hand-carved pews being used for seats in pubs.

☞

We must restore the nave to its former beauty

The same steps apply to the restoring of the nave. Side shrines and Stations of the Cross that have disappeared over the decades can be fashioned anew or purchased from antique dealers and architectural salvage companies. Yet sometimes the destruction of church interiors goes far beyond what was removed. In many cases, it's also what has been added. Wood paneling, drop ceilings with acoustical tiles, and wall-to-wall carpeting are the biggest offenders. Fortunately such materials date the project to the late '60s and '70s, when homeowners were renovating their houses in much the same fashion. The use of these cheap materials has dropped out of fashion, *Deo gratias*. The removal of such "homey" items will offend few.

Because these materials are so flimsy and impermanent, they're easily removed. With any luck, they'll have preserved what they were once hiding. The removal of ceiling tiles may reveal vaulting, clerestories, or ceiling murals intact and in good condition. Carpet removal can reveal terrazzo flooring or beautiful hardwood floorboards, and the removal of wood paneling can give way to beautiful plaster walls, sometimes decorated with beautiful stenciling or even mosaics.

More difficult to deal with, however, are the modern furnishings that replaced the traditional ones and are often at odds with the original design and style of the building. Victor Hugo dubbed these innovative furnishings the "wretched gewgaws of the day."

Referring to elements of the eighteenth-century renovation of Notre Dame Cathedral, he asked, "Who has substituted for the old Gothic altar, splendidly loaded with shrines and reliquaries, that heavy sarcophagus of marble, with angels' heads and clouds, which looks like an unmatched specimen from the Val-de-Grâce or Les Invalides!"[127]

In the late 1980s, historical St. Francis Xavier Church in Cincinnati was renovated: fashion audaciously fitted into the wounds of its Neo-Gothic architecture the wretched gewgaws of our own day: the interior of this immense church was painted a dark shade of blue to effect the look of marble, and the contemporary furnishings (altar, ambo, font, light fixtures, etc.) look as though they were transplanted from a mod-style library or a three-star hotel lobby. The contrast between the Gothic architectural forms (barrel vaults, pointed arches, and soaring columns) and the sharp, hard lines of the new fixtures creates an awkward visual dissonance that's disturbing even to the casual observer.

Seating is another major restoration item. First, in those churches that had the kneelers removed from the pews: install new kneelers! In those churches that have skewed or turned their side-aisle pews supposedly to allow people better to focus on the altar: turn them back facing forward. And in those churches that discarded the old pews in favor of cheap (or expensive) portable chairs, it would be ideal if new wooden pews with kneelers were eventually to be restored to the church. The fad of homey cushioned chairs will soon pass.

All in all, when restoring a historical church, the parish needs to hire competent restorationists with a proven track record of accomplishments. They must be sensitive to the original architecture of the church, but need not necessarily re-create exactly what existed some time in the past. Any new furnishings or artwork

---

[127] Hugo, *The Hunchback of Notre Dame*, 135.

introduced into the church, however, should be in keeping with the architectural scheme rather than looking like foreign invaders. The restorationist should be concerned with:

- reordering the church into a properly defined narthex, nave, and sanctuary in keeping with the original design;

- re-establishing an iconographic program of sacred art and furnishings;

- recovering any verticality that has been lost; and

- establishing a unified whole so that the church will be restored to a sacred place with transcendent qualities.

*We must build a sense of hierarchy
into poorly designed churches*

Some may say, "We're stuck with this ugly building that looks like a gymnasium. What can we do to improve on the modern design?" Fortunately, in some cases there's an easy answer.

In Edward Sövik's theory of the non-church, he expressed his desire for a building that has a "throwaway interior," that is, an interior that can be easily altered to suit the needs of the people at any time. Accordingly, the interiors of many of the non-churches built in the latter half of the twentieth century can be easily altered. Their throwaway interiors can simply be thrown away and new furnishings, and works of sacred art can be commissioned.

Of course, the new architect or designer has no obligation to subscribe to the modernist theory of the throwaway interior. On the contrary, he has the obligation of transforming the building into a beautiful church. It can be done, but not by designing another interior that can just be thrown away. The architect has the opportunity to reconnect with tradition to create a sacred place that will transcend generations and possibly cultures, too.

Some may say, "We're stuck with this ugly building that looks like a gymnasium. What can we do to improve on the modern design?" In the salvaging renovation of St. Aloysius Church (1960s) in New Canaan, Connecticut, architect Henry Hardinge Menzies took the opportunity to reconnect with tradition to create a sacred place that will transcend generations and possibly cultures, too. (Above — top: interior before renovation; bottom: interior after renovation. Facing page — top: exterior before renovation; bottom: exterior after renovation.)

Just as with the restoration project of a traditional church building, the first task in restoring a modern church is properly to reorient the interior spaces into a hierarchy of sanctuary and nave. This is more difficult to do with the modern edifice than with the traditional church building, because the floor plan may be somewhat irregular. Churches in-the-round, fan-shaped theater-style churches, and asymmetrical layouts are three popular arrangements that ought to be corrected.

In this regard, the altar needs to be established at the "head" of the building, in a distinct sanctuary that's elevated above the nave and set off from the congregational seating. Most likely the altar in the modern church to be renovated is unworthy to be used in the renovated church. The opportunity now exists to design a new altar that will not only establish itself as the focal point of the church, but will also set the tone for the new interior. Every other element of the renovation will lead to the altar in some way.

A new baldacchino or reredos can give the altar the nobility and prominence it deserves, and the close relationship of the tabernacle with the altar is just as important in the renovation of a modern edifice as it is in the restoration of a historical church. The same goes for other elements and furnishings — pews, sacred art, pulpit, and communion rail. There's no reason why the traditional trappings of a Catholic church can't be introduced into the modern building to create a sense of the transcendent and the eternal.

We must abandon churches that
can't be made to reflect the Faith

Of course, if it's possible, it's better to begin anew designing a church that can serve as a "city on a hill," one that through its traditional form and exterior elements has the capacity to carry meaning, to inspire, to educate, and to attract Catholics and non-Catholics alike. Since many or even most modern church edifices

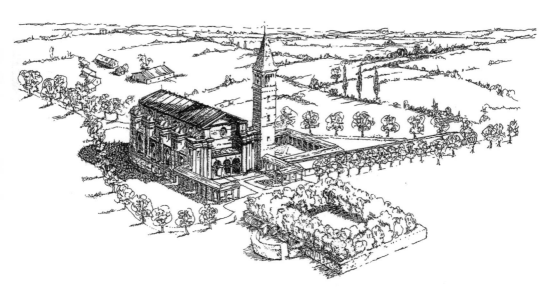

If it's possible, it's better to begin anew designing a church that can serve as a "city on a hill," one that through its traditional form and exterior elements has the capacity to carry meaning, to inspire, to educate, and to attract Catholics and non-Catholics alike. The new Immaculate Conception Church in Clinton, New Jersey, designed by Allan Greenberg, replaces the existing parish church. The design includes a prominent campanile, a colonnaded atrium, and other familiar church elements.

don't appear as permanent structures, their buildings can be adapted to another use, one that would serve the parish in another way — for instance, as a school building, food pantry, theater, gymnasium, or parish meeting hall.

Many of the modern churches, because of their layout and arrangement, lend themselves easily to such a transformation. Not a few people have entered one of these new churches or non-churches and exclaimed, "My, this looks more like a gymnasium [or a theater, etc.]!" If it looks like a gym or a theater, chances are it can easily be converted into a gym or theater while a new church, designed in continuity with the Catholic tradition of church architecture, rises nearby. These are properly called "replacement churches."

In fact, a pastor or bishop can easily save face by telling a parish that the current modern facility they're using as a church was serving only as a temporary solution until a time came when parishioners could help build a permanent house of God that would speak equally to generations of Catholics to come.

Finally, the greatest opportunity comes perhaps when a new parish is established. The pastor, architect, and parish can start at ground zero, so to speak. The parish has the great advantage of hindsight. It can look back over fifty years of ugly, uninspiring church designs to avoid building a fad that will pass away even before the current generation has died out. There's a unique opportunity to connect with the tradition of creating transcendent vessels of meaning that will not only look like churches but will be churches in their essence.

*We must hire architects
whose designs reflect the Faith*

For more than fifteen hundred years, the Church built splendid houses of God without the aid of so-called "experts" known as liturgical design consultants. Unfortunately, this new church professional, introduced in the twentieth century, has been the font of the failed experimentation. Such professionals, usually not trained in architecture and often not trained properly in the Liturgy, are simply the transmitters of the day's theological and liturgical fads. It's the LDC who insists that the baptismal font should be here or there, that the tabernacle can't possibly be near the altar, or that Catholics shouldn't kneel when they come to church.

When St. Agnes Church, near Grand Central Station in
New York City, incurred extensive fire damage in the early 1990s,
the church was rebuilt using classical forms. The tabernacle is built as part
of an altarpiece that's directly behind the new altar. A communion rail,
a raised pulpit, and side aisle shrines are other features of the new church.

It's also the LDC who has usurped the duties of the architect, without having the expertise of a trained architect. In many projects, the consultant forcibly presents his agenda and informs the architect how things will be done. The architect, in turn, is reduced to a pencil pusher who pushes the pencil the way the LDC says to push it. It's humiliating really! What if Borromini or Michelangelo were bossed around by an LDC? Their talents would have been suppressed, and they probably never would have continued to work on church projects. That's what has happened to many architects during the past forty years. Those who were not a part of the modern liturgical movement were summarily dismissed by self-appointed experts who wanted nothing more than to preach their own faddish philosophies, theologies, and design solutions.

The one sure way to perpetuate the crisis of ugly and dysfunctional Catholic church architecture is to ensure that LDCs continue to be placed in charge of such projects.

Yet not just any architect will do. The architect hired to design and oversee the construction of a Catholic church should be someone who understands the history and tradition of Catholic church architecture, not someone who wants to incorporate his own idiosyncratic theology in the design of a new church.

Unfortunately this has happened during recent years in some rather high-profile projects. Sometime in the '90s it became popular to spend an enormous amount of Church dollars to generate publicity regarding the construction of a new church or cathedral. Often a competition between name-brand architects was carried out. Yet these name brands had nothing to show in the way of previous accomplishments in building beautiful and useful church structures.

The first of these well-known competitions was for the "prototype" Millennium Church in Rome. Competitors included deconstructivist architects such as New York's Peter Eisenman, whose work often resembles train wrecks, and L.A.'s Richard Meier, who has never designed a building that wasn't white. Eisenman's design suggests that he knew little or nothing about the Catholic Church or her Liturgy, customs, and history. His submission depicted a sanctuary that was disconnected from the nave; in fact, the proposal appeared to place the nave and sanctuary in different buildings. Meier's winning scheme was a modernist monstrosity of glass and white "stuff." Instead of a tabernacle behind the altar, his scheme placed a giant television screen.

In a more high-profile project in the United States, name-brand architects vied for the commission to design the new Los Angeles Cathedral. Spanish architect Raphael Moneo won that heavily publicized competition, but the resultant building was far from a beautiful edifice despite its price tag of $163 million, which could have facilitated the design of several beautiful cathedrals. Many of the same architects competed for the commission to design the Oakland Cathedral. Swiss architect Santiago Calatrava, the winner in Oakland, produced a giant clamshell and told the international press that his design was based on the idea of creating something "totally independent of the Catholic Church."[128]

From the publicity generated by such competitions and experimental designs, you might think there's no architect today capable of designing a beautiful church that gives glory to God and can speak to ages beyond the present. This, however, simply isn't true. In fact, there's plenty of talent out there that has gone unused for the past half century.

One striking example comes from Thomas Michael Marano, when he was merely a student of architecture at the University of Notre Dame. In 1996 Marano produced designs for the Los Angeles cathedral competition. Comparisons of his traditional design

[128] Zahid Sardar, "Cathedral Dreams," *San Francisco Chronicle Magazine* (February 18, 2001).

with Moneo's built project is revealing. Marano's entry, with its beautiful iconographic façade, recognizable form, dome, rose window, and baldacchino, puts to shame Moneo's concrete monstrosity, which is not only unidentifiable as a Catholic cathedral but is by objective standards an ugly building.

Marano is one of many young architects who has graduated from Notre Dame's classical architecture program, the only such program offered by a Catholic college or university in the United States. In fact, it's one of the few classical programs offered at any school since the latter half of the twentieth century.

Under the guidance of architect Thomas Gordon Smith, who was hired by the university in 1989 to revamp its architecture program, students are exposed to the architectural theories and methods of ancient Greece and Rome, medieval Europe, and the Renaissance in order to understand the classical principles of architecture, principles that have long been dismissed or undermined by the architects of modernism and deconstruction. Such study of historical methods has produced a whirlwind of new interest in traditional church design. In turn, Notre Dame's program has proven that it can train architects who can responsibly design church buildings for the twenty-first century and beyond. Few if any of those graduating from Notre Dame are interested in creating church buildings that are "independent of the Catholic Church" let alone creating fads in the manner of the "non-church" promoted by Sövik and others of like mind. They're more interested in creating churches that are transcendent, well-built, elegant, enduring structures that can be understood by future generations of lay Catholics as well as by architects who will look to these designs to inform their own work.

One of Notre Dame's architecture professors, Duncan Stroik, established the Institute of Sacred Architecture to promote traditional church architecture beyond the walls of the university and the profession. The institute publishes a well-read journal called

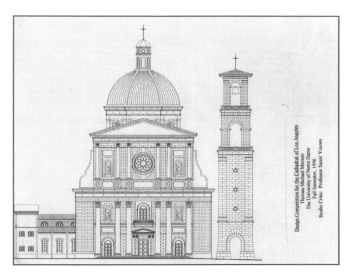

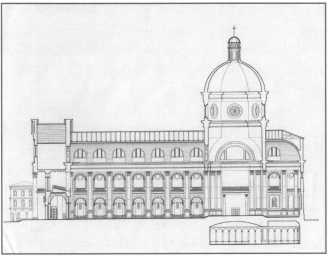

Design submitted in the Los Angeles Cathedral design competition. With its beautiful iconographic façade, recognizable form, dome baldacchino, and rose window, this design puts to shame the cathedral now under construction in Los Angeles, a concrete monstrosity that's not only unidentifiable as a Catholic church but is also by objective standards, simply an ugly building.

Sacred Architecture and has organized several exhibits in Rome of current work in the field of traditionally oriented church architecture. Interest in the Notre Dame program and the institute's offerings reflects renewed appreciation for understanding the works of the past in order to create new sacred architecture for the centuries to come. Even many Protestant architects are now interested in transforming uninspiring Protestant churches into more glorious structures that raise man's mind to God and to things eternal.

⌒

We must confidently build
churches that are truly Catholic

Despite common sense and evidence to the contrary, public opinion still holds that we can't build beautiful, timeless churches today. The reasons vary: there aren't talented architects and artists; Vatican II says our new churches must be modern and ugly; we can't afford to build enduring edifices as Christians of centuries past have always done; or there are better things to spend our money on, like feeding the poor and educating the young.

These reasons are simply popular misconceptions. In reality, the exact opposite holds true. First, we've just seen that there's an abundance of talented architects and artists today. Second, as explained in an earlier chapter, the Second Vatican Council didn't mandate or even suggest reforming Catholic church architecture. In fact, the council ratified the treasury of sacred art and architecture by calling for its proper preservation and maintenance. Unfortunately, because the ugly and dysfunctional churches as well as denuded ones seemed to crop up after the council, many people have mistakenly drawn the conclusion that the council somehow called for them. As the documents of Vatican II are being more widely read, more and more people, however, are discovering that many changes in the Church — including those in architecture, art, and Liturgy — don't have their origins or inspiration from the council, but, rather, that such changes were implemented by those who elected to follow their own agendas over what the council fathers envisioned and called for.

Second, stewardship of our Father's House falls equally to bishop, priest, and laity. Each has his own particular role and responsibility. If we were to think back a century or so and reflect on the splendid church edifices that were raised in God's honor, we would be ashamed. In the U.S. and Canada, for instance, cathedrals and parish churches of that era were built with the dimes of the Catholic working class, poor immigrants who often owned neither car nor house. There were few major patrons, such as in the days of Constantine, Charlemagne, or Justinian, and the fledgling Catholic Church in North America wasn't rich, as it is overwhelmingly today.

Just as Bezalel and Oholiab contributed their God-given talents to building the tabernacle in the wilderness,[129] artists, craftsmen, tradesmen, and even farmers contributed their time, talent, money, and natural resources to the building of a parish church. Farmers transported building materials to the site. Timber, sand, and gravel were donated and brought to town. Parishioners carted bricks to the construction site by their horses and wagons. And courageous men constructed tall church spires, often swinging in the breeze 100 or 150 feet above the church steps below until they successfully erected the cross atop the spire.

In the twenty-first century, at least in Europe and North America, we're blessed with an unprecedented abundance of resources. We're blessed with natural resources, and current technology assists in mining those resources in responsible, efficient ways. We're blessed with a talented, creative laity, albeit many lay members of the Church need to set their priorities straight and give glory to God rather than to themselves and to others.

[129] Cf. Exod. 31.

Right: Michael Imber's design proposal for the chapel at Thomas Aquinas College in Ojai, California.

Below: Our Lady of the Angels Monastery Chapel in Hanceville, Alabama.

From the publicity generated by such competitions and experimental designs, you might think there's no architect today capable of designing a beautiful church that gives glory to God and can speak to ages beyond the present. This, however, simply isn't true. In fact, there's plenty of talent out there that has gone unused.

Left: Design for Our Lady of the Most Holy Trinity in southern California.

Below: Thomas Gordon Smith's design for Our Lady of Guadalupe Seminary in Denton, Nebraska.

Ugly as Sin

We're also blessed with abundant financial resources. Never before in the history of the world have there been such prosperous nations. In fact, the surplus wealth among lay Catholics is so great that the stewardship of material patrimony will in no way detract from stewardship in other areas of Catholic life, such as feeding the poor, educating priests, forming religious, and performing the spiritual and corporal works of mercy in a most generous way.

⌒

The Vatican wants us to do this

Bishops and priests, who are charged with the duty to protect the Church's material patrimony, bear a unique responsibility. In addition to establishing sacred places, their responsibility entails preserving the house of God and its sacred furnishings — art, vessels, linens, and vestments. It's worth reiterating that, according to *Sacrosanctum Concilium*, Vatican II's Constitution on the Sacred Liturgy, ". . . in the course of the centuries [the Church] has brought into being a treasury of art which must be carefully preserved." As mentioned in an earlier chapter, bishops are warned that they "must be very careful to see that sacred furnishings and works of value are not disposed of or allowed to deteriorate; for they are the house of God."[130] A few years later, the Vatican reiterated the importance of this pronouncement in a short document on the care and preservation of the Church's historical and artistic patrimony, *Opera Artis:*

> Disregarding the warnings and legislation of the Holy See, many people have made unwarranted changes in places of worship under the pretext of carrying out the reform of the Liturgy and thus have caused the disfigurement or loss of priceless works of art. Mindful of the legislation of Vatican

---

[130] *Sacrosanctum Concilium*, no. 123.

Council II and of the directives in the documents of the Holy See, bishops are to exercise unfailing vigilance to ensure that the remodeling of places of worship by reason of the reform of the Liturgy is carried out with utmost caution.

The Vatican here makes explicit that unnecessary and unwanted renovations of Catholic churches and cathedrals aren't proper stewardship of God's house.

Bishops, priests, and the laity must work together to maintain the sacred places that our ancestors in the Faith have built, and we must continue to establish new churches that are equally or surpassingly beautiful and sacred edifices. We are all called to be responsible stewards of our Father's house.

⌒

It takes only six simple steps

Just as the alcoholic's first step to recovery is admitting that he has a problem, the first step toward a renewal of sacred architecture is the willingness to admit that the ugly and dysfunctional churches of the post-Vatican II years are just that: ugly and dysfunctional, banal and uninspiring.

The second step is to identify the source of the problem: those with theological agendas who wish to change the face of Catholicism, how people worship, and ultimately what they believe.

The third step is to remove the cancer: the modern church professional known as the liturgical design consultant needs to be eliminated from the host of characters required to renovate or build a church.

The fourth step is to identify and employ properly trained architects who are capable of fulfilling the task to build houses of God that will raise man's heart and mind to God and to things eternal, architects and artists who are willing to employ the natural laws of church architecture and to look to the past to inform their own designs, which will in turn inspire the work of future church builders.

The fifth step is for bishops, priests, and laity to commit themselves to a plan of stewardship that will allow the architects and designers to establish and preserve these sacred places using the finest materials reasonably available.

The final step should be the ongoing education of seminarians, priests, and laity about the meaning and significance of the church building and its intimate relationship to the Catholic Faith.

We can bring about a renaissance of sacred architecture

Let us return to Victor Hugo's *Hunchback of Notre Dame*. Inspired by Hugo's novel, which criticized what Parisians of the eighteenth century had done to the great cathedral in the name of fashion, architect Eugène Emmanuel Viollet-le-Duc drew up a plan to restore the cathedral to its former splendor. He created stained-glass windows by copying stained glass from the cathedrals in other French cities that had escaped the fashion-driven, school-trained architects and the indiscriminate destruction wrought by the Revolution.

He also replaced all the sculptures; he researched the pictorial records of other French Gothic cathedrals, and by doing so, he was able to re-create the works of the medieval sculptors. He designed a new flèche to top off the crossing of the cathedral as it had once been. He also restored the great doors of the cathedral and the gargoyles on the rooftop. Finally, he had the interior scoured of the old whitewash and treated the exterior with a chemical that would preserve the stone from the industrial pollution that was already becoming a problem in the nineteenth century.

Thus, Viollet-le-Duc took on one of the greatest projects in the history of restoration and was successful in returning Notre Dame Cathedral to its original beauty and charm. Similarly, in the twenty-first century, if Catholics are willing to admit that the experiments of the twentieth century are failures, and if they're motivated to correct the situation, a renaissance of sacred architecture will take hold whereby we'll see the great treasures of the past returned to their original splendor and the establishment of new houses of God that are transcendent, enduring, and serve as vessels of meaning for generations of Christians to come.

Appendix

References and resources
for further research

The following is a bibliography of authoritative Church documents that address in some way matters of church architecture, design, or renovation. Useful for parishioners, pastors, building-committee members, and architects, these documents present the Church's teaching on church art and architecture.

Divini Cultus, Apostolic Constitution on Divine Worship, Pope Pius XI, 1928.

Mediator Dei, Encyclical on the Sacred Liturgy, Pope Pius XII, 1947.

Sacrosanctum Concilium, Vatican II's Constitution on the Sacred Liturgy, 1963.

Sacram Liturgiam, Motu Proprio on the Sacred Liturgy, Pope Paul VI, 1964.

Inter Oecumenici, Instruction on the Proper Implementation of the Constitution on the Sacred Liturgy, approved by Pope Paul VI, 1964.

Tres Abhinc Annos, Second Instruction on the Proper Implementation of the Constitution on the Sacred Liturgy, approved by Pope Paul VI, 1967.

Eucharisticum Mysterium, Instruction on the Worship of the Eucharistic Mystery, Pope Paul VI, 1967.

Liturgicae Instaurationes, Third Instruction on the Correct Implementation of the Constitution on the Sacred Liturgy, Pope Paul VI, 1970.

Opera Artis, Circular Letter on the Care of the Church's Historical and Artistic Heritage, Sacred Congregation for the Clergy, approved by Pope Paul VI, 1971.

Eucharistiae Sacramentum, On Holy Communion and the Worship of the Eucharist Outside of Mass, Pope Paul VI, 1973.

Dedication of a Church and an Altar, Sacred Congregation for Divine Worship, 1977.

Dominicae Cenae, On the Mystery and Worship of the Eucharist, Pope John Paul II, 1980.

Inaestimabile Donum, Instruction on Certain Norms Concerning the Worship of the Eucharistic Mystery, Sacred Congregation for Divine Worship, approved by Pope John Paul II, 1980.

Code of Canon Law, approved by Pope John Paul II, 1983.

Duodecimum Saeculum, On representations and imagery, Pope John Paul II, 1987.

Love Your Mass, Apostolic Letter on the 25th anniversary of *Sacrosanctum Concilium*, Pope John Paul II, 1988.

Catechism of the Catholic Church, approved by Pope John Paul II, 1994.

Ecclesiae de Mysterio, On certain questions regarding the collaboration of the non-ordained faithful in the sacred ministry of priests, approved by Pope John Paul II, 1997.

Apostolos Suos, On the limitations of national episcopal conferences, Pope John Paul II, 1998.

Letter to Artists, Pope John Paul II, 1999.

❧

Resources on church architecture

The following journals, articles, books, and websites pertain to church architecture. The church architecture of the present and future ought to, in the words of *Sacrosanctum Concilium,* "grow organically from forms already existing." The resources included in this section serve as visual and textual sources for church architecture. Few of them require special education or technical knowledge to make them useful for new church design or renovation. Many of the books listed here provide an excellent array of images that explain the various traditional arrangements of churches. Others provide a sampling of beautiful twentieth-century churches that can be used for inspiring church designs of the twenty-first century.

❧

Recommended Journals

Sacred Architecture, P.O. Box 556, Notre Dame, IN 46556; (219) 631-5762; Editor: Duncan Stroik; e-mail: dstroik@nd.edu.

Adoremus Bulletin, P.O. Box 3286, St. Louis, MO 63130; (314) 863-8385; Editor: Helen Hull Hitchcock; www.adoremus.org.

Christifidelis, Newsletter for the St. Joseph Foundation, 11107 Wurzbach, #601B, San Antonio, TX 78230-2553; 210-697-0717; Director: Charles M. Wilson; www.st-joseph-foundation.org.

❧

Internet Resources

The Catholic Liturgical Library: www.catholicliturgy.com; Editor: Ian Rutherford; e-mail: webmaster@catholicliturgy.com.

Domus Dei — The House of God: www.domus-dei.org; e-mail: domusdei@mindspring.com.

⁂

Salvage Companies — Church Art and Furnishings

Architectural Antiques and Salvage, 31 South Richmond St., Porto-
bello Bridge, Dublin 2, Ireland; phone: (01) 478 4245; fax: (01)
475 8708; e-mail: thebirdflan@hotmail.com.

Church Connection, 216 Cumer Road, McDonald, PA 15057;
phone: (866) 873-3735; e-mail: into@usedchurchitems.com;
www.usedchurchitems.com.

Chancellor's Church Furnishings, Rivernook Farm, Sunnyside,
Walton-on-Thames, England; phone: +44 (0) 1932 252736;
e-mail: info@churchantiques.com; www.churchantiques.com.

Church Furnishings Clearinghouse, Kenneth T. Pribanic: phone: (202)
723-7452; fax: (202) 723-7453; www.churchclearinghouse.com.

Neville Griffiths Antiques and Interiors, 5 New St., Lower
Weedon, Northamptonshire, NN7 4QS, England; e-mail:
nevillegriffiths@talk21.com; www.nevillegriffiths.com.

⁂

Books

Adams, Henry. *Mont-Saint-Michel and Chartres*. Cambridge, MA:
The Riverside Press, 1904.

Anson, Peter. *Churches, Their Plan and Furnishing*. Milwaukee:
Bruce Publishing Co., 1948.

Aubert, Marcel. *French Cathedral Windows*. New York: Oxford
University Press, 1947.

Borromeo, St. Charles. *Instructions on Ecclesiastical Buildings*. Evelyn
Carol Voelker, trans. Dissertation, Syracuse University, 1979.

Brannach, Frank. *Church Architecture: Building for a Living Faith*, 1932.

Collins, Msgr. Harold E. *The Church Edifice and Its Appointments*, 1925.

Comes, John T. *Catholic Art and Architecture: A Lecture to Seminarists*, 1920.

Conant, Kenneth John. *Carolingian and Romanesque Architecture 800-1200*. Baltimore: Penguin Books, 1959.

Cram, Ralph Adams. *Church Building*. Boston: Marshall Jones Co., 1924.

Cram, Ralph Adams. *The Ministry of Art*, 1914.

Cram, Ralph Adams. *American Church Building of Today*, 1929.

Didron, Alphonse Napoleon. *Christian Iconography: The History of Christian Art in the Middle Ages* (2 volumes). New York: Fredrick Ungar Publishing Co., 1965.

Elliot, Msgr. Peter J. *Ceremonies of the Modern Roman Rite*. San Francisco: Ignatius Press, 1995.

Elliot, Msgr. Peter J. *Liturgical Question Box*. San Francisco: Ignatius Press, 1998.

Fletcher, Sir Banister. A *History of Architecture on the Comparative Method*. London: B. T. Batsford Ltd., 1896.

Frankl, Paul. *Gothic Architecture*. Baltimore: Penguin Books, 1967.

Gill, Eric. *Beauty Looks After Herself*. London: Sheed and Ward, 1933.

Grabar, Andre. *Christian Iconography: A Study of Its Origins*. Princeton, NJ: Princeton University Press, 1968.

Grodecki, Louis. *Gothic Architecture*. New York: Abrams, 1976.

Hammett, Ralph Warner. *The Romanesque Architecture of Western Europe*. New York: The Architectural Book Publishing Co., 1927.

Jones, E. Michael. *Living Machines*. San Francisco: Ignatius Press, 1995.

Kraus, Henry. *The Living Theatre of Medieval Art*. Bloomington, IN: Indiana University Press, 1967.

Krautheimer, Richard. *Early Christian and Byzantine Architecture*. Baltimore: Penguin Books, 1965.

Kubach, Hans Erich. *Romanesque Architecture*. New York: Abrams, 1972.

Kubler, George, and Soria, Martin. *Art and Architecture in Spain and Portugal 1500-1800*. Baltimore: Penguin Books, 1959.

Lee, Lawrence; Seldon, George; and Stephens, Francis. *Stained Glass*. New York: Crown Publishers, Inc., 1976.

Lowrie, Walter. *Art in the Early Church*. New York: Pantheon Books, 1947.

Mango, Cyril. *Byzantine Architecture*. New York: Abrams, 1974.

Martindale, Andrew. *Gothic Art from the Twelfth to Fifteenth Century*. New York: Fredrick A. Praeger, Inc. Publishers, 1967.

Mitchel, Ann. *Cathedrals of Europe*. Norwich, UK: Hanlyn Publishing Group Limited, 1968.

Murray, Peter. *Renaissance Architecture*. New York: Abrams, 1971.

Norberg-Schulz, *Christian. Late Baroque and Rococo Architecture*. New York: Abrams, 1971.

Portoghesi, Paolo. *The Rome of Borromini: Architecture as Language*. New York: George Braziller, Inc., 1967.

Rose, Michael S. *The Renovation Manipulation: The Church Counter-Renovation Handbook*. Cincinnati: Aquinas Publishing Ltd., 2000.

Rosponi, Christiano. *Reconquering Sacred Space: Rediscovering Tradition in Twentieth-Century Liturgical Architecture*. Rome: Il Bosco E La Nave, 1999.

Rosponi, Christiano. *Reconquering Sacred Space 2000: The Church in the City of the Third Millennium*. Rome: Il Bosco E La Nave, 2000.

Schloeder, Steven J. *Architecture in Communion*. San Francisco: Ignatius Press, 1998.

Short, Ernest, ed. *Post War Church Building: A Practical Handbook*. London: Hollis and Carter, 1947.

Smith, Thomas Gordon. *Classical Architecture: Rule and Invention*. Layton, UT: G.M. Smith, 1988.

Stoddard, Whitney S. *The West Portals of Saint-Denis and Chartres*. Cambridge, MA: Harvard University Press, 1952.

Suger, Abbot. *The Abbey Church of St.-Denis and Its Art Treasures*. E. Panofsky, trans. Princeton, NJ: Princeton University Press, 1979.

Tapie, Victor-L. *The Age of Grandeur: Baroque Art and Architecture*. New York: Grove Press, Inc., 1957.

Temko, Allan. *Notre-Dame of Paris: The Biography of a Cathedral*. New York: The Viking Press, 1955.

Volbach, W. F. *Early Christian Art*. New York: Abrams (no date).

Von Simson, Otto. *The Gothic Cathedral: Origins of Gothic Architecture and the Medieval Concept of Order*. New York: Harper and Row, 1964.

Webb, Geoffrey. *Architecture in Britain: The Middle Ages*. Baltimore: Penguin Books, Inc., 1956.

Weber, Edward J. *Catholic Church Buildings: Their Planning and Furnishing*, 1927.

Wilson, Christopher. *The Gothic Cathedral: The Architecture of the Great Church 1130-1530*. London: Thames and Hudson Ltd., 1990.

Wittkower, Rudolf. *Art and Architecture in Italy 1600-1750*. Baltimore: Penguin Books, 1958.

Recommended architects and artists

Following is a list of some architects and artists who understand the Church's architectural patrimony and are committed to traditional Catholic church architecture as outlined in the present work. This ought to be an excellent resource for dioceses and parish building committees when it comes time to find an architect. North American, European, and Asian architects are included.

North America

Angelo Alberto, 3801 Kennett Pike, D , Wilmington, DE 19807; phone: (302) 376-6450; fax: (302) 376-6460; e-mail: aatownplan@aol.com.

H. Reed Armstrong, 13 Sussex Rd., Silver Spring, MD 20910; phone: (301) 585-4456; fax: (301) 608-0532.

John Blatteau, 1930 Chestnut St., #5, Philadelphia, PA 19103; phone: (215) 751-9779; fax: (215) 751-0734; e-mail: doric@pobox.upenn.edu.

John Burgee, Architect, 1592 E. Mountain Dr., Montecito, CA 93108; phone/fax: (805) 969-5239.

Lio Casas and Michael Mesko, Curtis and Windham, 3701 Travis St., Houston, TX 77002.

Ugly as Sin

Andrés Duany and Elizabeth Plater-Zyberk, DPZ Architects,
    1023 SW 25th Ave., Miami, FL 33135; phone: (305) 644-1023;
    fax: (305) 644-102.

Robert Goodall, 1300 Spring St., Silver Spring, MD 20910;
    phone: (301) 588-4800.

William Heyer and Selena Heyer, 125 West Marion St., #116,
    South Bend, IN 46601; (219) 251-0649; (219) 287-0821.

Carter Hord, 80 Monroe, #102, Memphis, TN 38103; phones:
    (901) 527-9085; (703) 739-3845; fax: (703) 739-3846.

Michael Imber, 111 W. El Prado, San Antonio, TX 78212;
    phone: (210) 824-7703.

Dennis H. Keefe, Keefe Associates, Inc., 162 Boylston St., Boston,
    MA 02116; phone: (617) 482-5859; fax: (617) 482-7321.

James Langley, Department of Fine Arts, Franciscan University,
    100 Franciscan Way, Steubenville, OH 43952; phone: (614)
    282-3904; fax: (614) 283-6401.

Jonathan Lee, 311½ Howard St., Petoskey, MI 49770; phone:
    (231) 487-0089; fax: (231) 487-9911.

Dino Marcantonio, 110 Bond Hall, School of Architecture,
    University of Notre Dame, Notre Dame, IN 46556; phone:
    (219) 631-4451.

Henry Hardinge, Menzies, Architect, 99 Overlook Cir., New
    Rochelle, NY 10804; phone: (914) 235-0198; fax: (914)
    235-7805; e-mail: hmenzies@aol.com.

James McCrery, 625 E. Capitol St., N.E., Washington, DC 20003;
    phone: (205) 588-0700.

Duncan McRoberts, 150 Lake St. South, Ste. 208, Kirkland,
    WA 98033.

Paul Milana, Cooper Robertson Partners, 311 West 43 St., New
    York, NY 10036; phone: (212) 247-1717; fax: (212) 245-0361.

Recommended architects and artists

Stefan Molina, Turner Boaz Stocker, 301 N. Market St., Ste. 200, Dallas, TX 75206; phone: (214) 761-9465.

Edward Mudd, 23 Park Pl., New Canaan, CT 06840.

Kevin Roche, 20 Davis St., Hamden, CT 06517; phone: (203) 777-7251; fax: (203) 776-2299.

Rolf Rohn, Architect, 5075 Clairton Blvd., Ste. 301, Pittsburgh, PA 15236; phone: (412) 561-1228.

Steven Schloeder, Liturgical Environs, 2510 Le Conte, #105, Berkeley, CA 94709; phone/fax: (510) 666-9120; e-mail: litenv@hotmail.com.

Steven Semes, Cooper Robertson Partners, 311 West 43 St., New York, NY 10036; phone: (212) 247-1717; fax: (212) 245-0361.

Thomas Gordon Smith, 2025 Edison Rd., South Bend, IN 46637; office phone: (219) 287-1498; school phone: (219) 631-6137; office fax: (219) 287-0821; school fax: (219) 631-8486.

Duncan G. Stroik, University of Notre Dame, School of Architecture, 110 Bond Hall, Notre Dame, IN 46556; office phone: (219) 271-0522; school phone: (219) 631-5762; fax: (219) 631-8486; e-mail: dstroik@nd.edu.

John Tittmann, 58 Winter St., Boston, MA 02108; phone: (617) 451-5740; fax: (617) 451-2309; e-mail: artarch@wn.net.

David Vatter, Architect, 603 Olympia Rd., Pittsburgh, PA 15211; phone/fax: (412) 431-4245.

Stephen Wiseman, 311½ Howard St., Petoskey, MI 49770; phone: (231) 487-0089; fax: (231) 487-9911.

❧

Europe and Asia

Pier Carlo Bontempi, Studio Bontempi Strada Nazionale 96C, 43030 Gaiano di Collecchio, Italy; phone: (011) 390-521-80-9900.

Ugly as Sin

Piotr Choynowski, B. Farmanns GT. MB, 0271 Oslo, Norway;
  phones: (011) 47-22-55-2114; (011) 47-22-566-9777;
  fax: (011) 47-22-552-114.

José Cornelio da Silva, Colares 2710 Sintra, Portugal; phone:
  (011) 3511-888-2657.

Anthony Delarue Associates, 22 Lonsdale Square, London
  N1 1EN, Great Britain; phone: (011) 0171-700-0241;
  fax: (011) 0171-700-0242.

Michael Fuchs, A-3400 Klosterneuberg, Hermannstrasse 12, Austria;
  phone: (011) 43-2243-253-82; e-mail: M.Fuchs@michael-fuchs.

Jan Maciag, Maple Tree Cottage, New Road, Orton
  Waterville, Peterborough PE2 5EJ, Great Britain; phones:
  (011) 440-1733-230816; (011) 440-1733-391661; e-mail:
  113125.2240@compuserve.com.

David Mayernik, Roma, Italy; phone: (011) 39-06-689-2626;
  e-mail: jtmayernik@ibm.net.

José Narciso, Asian Architects, Room 202 SEDCCO Bldg.,
  120 Rada St., Legaspi Vill., Makati, Metro Manila, Philippines.

Helmut Peuker, Ainmillerstrasse 25, 80801 München, Germany.

Cristiano Rosponi, Via Muzio Attendolo 65, 00176 Roma, Italy;
  phone: (011) 39-06-214-8050; e-mail: roscri@flashnet.it.

Glossary of church architecture terms

apse: a semicircular extension of a church building; a central apse would serve as the back of the sanctuary.

altarpiece: a painted or carved image or images depicting the dedication of a church, e.g., St. Sebastian, the Annunciation, the Sacred Heart; this is either hung on the wall behind the altar or attached to the back of the altar itself.

altar rail: a low wall, usually balustraded, which distinguishes the sanctuary from the nave; also known as a "communion rail"; here communicants kneel to receive the Eucharist.

altar stone: a flat, solid piece of natural stone on which the priest places the Host and chalice during the Holy Sacrifice of the Mass; it's consecrated by the bishop and marked with five crosses, symbolizing the five wounds of Christ; the altar stone is placed on the surface of the altar.

ambo: an elevated lectern used for reading the Scriptures during liturgical ceremonies; traditionally the ambo has a flight of steps on both sides rising to a platform large enough to accommodate the reader and the candle-bearers.

arcade: a row of arches supported on columns, piers, or pilasters and usually roofed; used in church architecture since the early Christian basilicas.

atrium: an exterior forecourt to a church usually surrounded by a cloister.

baldacchino, baldachin: a permanent ornamental canopy constructed of wood, stone, or metal that's placed over the main altar in a church; it's typically supported by columns and has a dome- or crown-like top.

balustrade: a row of upright supports, usually vase-shaped posts or columns, topped by a rail.

basilica: a church that has a long, rectangular nave that leads to a circular apse containing the altar at the head of the structure; the basilica is often extended by transepts that project from the nave on either side.

bas-relief: a sculptural relief that projects very little from the flat background; in church it's usually hung on a wall or a column.

buttress, flying: a projecting arched structure used in Gothic churches such as Notre Dame de Paris to transfer the weight of the ceiling to the ground; this allows for the walls to be pierced with large areas of glazing.

campanile: a freestanding bell tower made popular by Italian church architecture; campaniles are typically square in plan, although some, such as the famous tower of Pisa, are circular towers.

cathedra: a bishop's throne in his cathedral church.

chancel: the area of the sanctuary reserved to the clergy and servers who are assisting the officiating priest or bishop; usually the front part of the sanctuary nearest the nave.

clerestory: (pronounced "clear-story") the upper part of the nave walls that usually contains small windows that admit light but no view because of their high placement.

cloister: a covered passageway, usually colonnaded, that encloses a space such as an atrium.

colonnade: a series of regularly spaced columns usually supporting the base of a roof.

cornice: a horizontal, molded projection that completes a building or a wall.

crossing: the space where the nave crosses the transepts; often articulated with a dome.

cruciform plan: a floor plan laid out in the form of a cross; the arms of the cross are formed by projecting transepts.

crypt: an underground burial place of a saint, typically beneath the altar or the nave of a church.

cupola: a small dome surmounting a roof; or the underside of a dome, the ceiling of a dome.

façade: the main face of a church, decorated with religious imagery.

flèche: a spire placed over the crossing of a church.

fresco: a wall painting that is executed on freshly spread plaster with water-soluble pigments.

gallery: a rear balcony that projects out over the nave.

lantern: a small tower, usually the uppermost part of a cupola or dome, that's used for ornamentation or projecting light; its form resembles that of a handheld lantern.

lintel: the horizontal beam over the head of a doorway or lintel; in church architecture, the lintel is often used as a decorative surface.

martyrium, martyrion: a small chapel or church built to commemorate the place where a martyr was killed or buried.

mosaic: a wall decoration made by fitting together small pieces of colored tiles.

narthex: the interior front entrance of a church that serves as a transition from the profane world outside to the sacred of the church interior.

nave: the main space of a church, which accommodates the congregation and extends from the front entrance to the sanctuary.

oculus: a round eye-like window or other opening; often found in a central location on the façade above the main doors of a church.

piazza: an open-air plaza of which the church façade serves as a backdrop; the area is used for civic, mercantile, and religious purposes.

pier: a vertical support at either end of an arch.

pilaster: a column, usually rectangular, that projects from a wall.

pillar: a freestanding column that serves as a building support.

pinnacle: a small spire on top of a buttress.

portal: a door opening into a church, or, more specifically, the decorative areas that surround the doors, especially above.

portico: a covered porch or walkway, usually supported by columns, that leads to the main entrance of the church.

pulpit: an elevated decorative stand in which one preaches; it typically has low walls on all sides except for the entrance from the stairwell.

reredos: an ornamental screen of painted panels or carved statues, placed behind and above the main altar in a church; the reredos often contains niches for statues.

retablo, retable: a shelf behind an altar used for supporting decorative works of sacred art, the altar crucifix, and liturgical candles.

rose window: large circular windows in church façades; it's typically made up of different sections of stained glass that resemble the petals of a flower.

spire: a tapering tower that crowns a steeple or surmounts the church.

transept: arm-like extensions of the interior of a cruciform church on either side of the nave near the sanctuary.

triumphal arch: the portion of the wall over the arch that divides the nave from the sanctuary.

tympanum: the area above the lintel of a doorway that's enclosed in an arch; often used for decorative portal sculpture.

⌒

Photo credits

Page 85: Altar, Holy Family, Dayton, Ohio: Michael S. Rose

Page 89: Baldacchino, St. Paul, New York: Michael S. Rose

Page 90: Reredos, St. Francis, Petoskey, Michigan: Troy Frantz

Page 93: Crucifix with St. John and Mary: Art Today

Page 95: Tabernacle, Sacred Heart, New York: Michael S. Rose

Chapter Three

Page 99: Façade, St. John, West Chester, Ohio: Michael S. Rose

Page 101: Entrance, St. Charles Borromeo, Kettering, Ohio: Michael S. Rose

Page 102: Entrance, St. Robert Bellarmine, Cincinnati (upper left); entrance, St. Ignatius, Cincinnati (lower right): Michael S. Rose

Page 104: Gathering space, St. Antoninus, Cincinnati: Michael S. Rose

Page 107: Font, St. John, West Chester, Ohio: Michael S. Rose

Page 109: Interior, St. John, West Chester, Ohio: Michael S. Rose

Page 113: Seating, St. John, West Chester, Ohio (top); nave, Our Lady of Lourdes, Cincinnati (bottom): Michael S. Rose

Page 116: Sanctuary, St. Robert Bellarmine, Cincinnati: Michael S. Rose

Page 120: Stations, St. Charles Borromeo, Kettering, Ohio: Michael S. Rose

Page 121: Crucifix, St. Robert Bellarmine, Cincinnati: Michael S. Rose

Page 124: Crucifix, St. Joseph, Trenton, Michigan: Jay McNally

Page 126: Sanctuary, St. Cyprian, Riverview, Michigan: Jay McNally

Page 127: Sanctuary, St. Charles Borromeo, Kettering, Ohio: Michael S. Rose

Ugly as Sin

Page 169: Exterior, St. Charles Borromeo, Kettering, Ohio:
Michael S. Rose

Chapter Five

Page 177: Notre Dame College chapel, Baltimore: Notre Dame College

Page 179: St. Mary, Rockford, Illinois: Institute of Christ the King
Sovereign Priest

Page 181: St. Paul, Worcester, Massachusetts (top): *Worcester
Telegram and Gazette*
St. Paul, Worcester, Massachusetts (bottom): Rohn
Design Group

Page 183: Warwick House Chapel, Pittsburgh: Jon Beckett

Page 189: Sanctuary, St. Aloysius, New Canaan, Connecticut:
Fred George

Page 194: Renovations, St. Aloysius, New Canaan, Connecticut:
Fred George

Page 195: Renovations, St. Aloysius, New Canaan, Connecticut:
Fred George

Page 197: Birdseye view, Immaculate Conception, Clinton, New
Jersey: Duncan Stroik

Page 199: St. Agnes, New York: Michael S. Rose

Page 203: Thomas Michael Marano's Los Angeles Cathedral
design: Duncan Stroik

Page 206: Michael Imber's design for Thomas Aquinas College chapel,
Ojai, California (top); Our Lady of the Angels Monastery
Chapel, Hanceville, Alabama (bottom): Duncan Stroik

Page 207: Design for Our Lady of the Most Holy Trinity in
southern California (top): Duncan Stroik
Design for Our Lady of Guadalupe Seminary, Denton,
Nebraska (bottom): Thomas Gordon Smith

Michael S. Rose

Michael Rose is uniquely qualified to lead the movement for the restoration of the Church's grand heritage of sacred architecture. Thoroughly trained in both architecture and the fine arts, he has an impressive command of the Church's liturgical tradition and a detailed awareness of how physical surroundings determine the nature of worship.

Rose holds a bachelor's degree in architecture from the University of Cincinnati and a master's degree in fine arts from Brown University.

As editor of *St. Joseph Messenger* and *St. Catherine Review*, and as a speaker, Rose indefatigably leads the fight for Catholic beauty and truth in architecture. The author of the book *The Renovation Manipulation*, he writes frequently and compellingly on sacred architecture; his articles have appeared in many periodicals, including *Envoy*, *New Oxford Review*, *National Catholic Register*, *Homiletic and Pastoral Review*, *Adoremus Bulletin*, *Lay Witness*, *Sacred Architecture*, *The Wanderer*, and *Culture Wars*.

With his thorough knowledge of art and architecture and his great devotion to the Catholic Faith, Rose shows readers why proper liturgical art and architecture is essential in Catholic churches: it raises man's soul to God and his mind to the things of Heaven.